Just One More Thing
Before You Leave Home

by
David Gudgel

with
Bernice Gudgel

JUST ONE MORE THING: BEFORE YOU LEAVE HOME
Copyright © 2013 David Gudgel
Printed by CreateSpace
www.createspace.com

Library of Congress Cataloging-in-Publication Data
Gudgel, David R.
Just one more thing: before you leave home / David R. Gudgel, with Bernice Gudgel.
Includes bibliographical references.

ISBN-10: 1484820584
ISBN-13:978-1484820582

To Brent, Brian, and Katie.
You made us what we are—happy parents.
Thanks for turning out great!

Contents

PART EIGHT: Painful Experiences

PART NINE: Spiritual Commitments

PART TEN: Practical Tips

Seriously...

Before You Leave Home

THERE ARE FOUR WORDS that I probably heard my parents say a million times when I was growing up. And strangely, they were four words that usually didn't really mean what they should have meant. I'm guessing you've probably heard them a few times from your parents too. *Just. One. More. Thing.*

I usually heard them when I was just about ready to leave the house to go out somewhere. Or when my parents were heading out the door to go somewhere. Sometimes I would even hear them when I was just going from one room to the next!

> "Oh David, *just one more thing* before you go. Can you take the trash bag from the kitchen out to the garbage on your way out? Thanks. Oh… and be sure to put gas in the car on your way home later. I won't have time to get it in the morning… And don't forget your coat!"

Just *one* more thing. Right.

"Okay kids, we'll be back by 9. Oh wait...*just one more thing.* Make sure you finish your homework before you watch tv or play video games. I'm serious!.. And don't have any friends come over while we're gone… And if you don't want to get up early enough to take a shower in the morning, take it tonight!"

"*Just one more thing…* can you bring me a soda from the kitchen since you're up? Oh and that magazine that's on the counter?"

It seemed like my parents always had *just one more thing* to tell me. It used to drive me crazy. It wasn't until I became a parent myself that I realized they weren't doing it just to annoy me.

As a parent I finally understood that there are a ton of things involved in raising kids. It amazes me sometimes that God even gives us the responsibility to do it! So many things to think about and to keep track of and to do. Helping your kids grow up to be safe and happy and prepared to live a productive life on their own is not easy! So we give it our best shot. And a lot of it comes out in words. Just one more thing…

When I was in high school, I started reading the Bible regularly. I used the Living Bible because it was easy to read and understand. Someone must have suggested I start with Proverbs, so that's what I did. If you haven't read that book, you should. It's loaded with practical advice about life.

Solomon, a king who is known as being the wisest man who ever lived, wrote proverbs. He wrote it as a book of advice to his son. It's divided into 31 chapters, so when I started reading it I read a chapter a day. I'd read the chapter that matched up with the date. And after I read through the whole book, I started it again on the first of the next month. And I kept doing that for a long time.

I still have that Bible and the book of Proverbs especially is all marked up with underlining and notes in the margins. Reading it gave me some much-needed help and began significantly changing me. Actually, the more I read, the better person I became. The practical help that Solomon wrote out for his son was also a big help to me.

Though Bernice and I can't claim to be as wise as Solomon was (well, I guess we could claim to be but it wouldn't be true) we too wanted to make sure that we had done our best to prepare our kids for life on their own. We did our best to be a good example to them, and to make sure they learned things they would need to know, and gave them experiences that would help them discover who God had uniquely created them to be.

As our oldest son, Brent, reached his mid high school years and started checking out colleges, we realized just how quickly those "18 years of child raising" were going by. And they were almost over! Pretty soon Brent would be out on his own. Had we done enough? Had we done it right? Was he ready?

We began praying about how to find that out.

Bernice and I are both list people. When we're trying to figure something out, or when we're planning something, we make lists. So we decided to make a list of some of the things—the big things —that we wanted to make sure Brent had gotten over the years. From our example, or family devotions, or Sunday School classes, or whatever. If we were to stop him on his way out the door to college and say "Oh wait Brent, just one more thing…" what would those things be? Had his training in this list of important things stuck? Had he really gotten it?

So we came up with our list, but we didn't want to lecture him on those things. We were pretty sure he wouldn't be crazy about that idea. So we decided to put together a binder with a short chapter on each of the topics from our list. Each chapter had some basic information and then some questions or Bible verses to think about.

Then we approached him with the bribe... I mean plan. If he was willing, he and dad would each do a chapter on their own every couple of weeks and then we'd go out to a late breakfast on Saturday together and discuss it. He was willing. So every couple weeks during Brent's senior year we would head out for breakfast with our binders and we'd sit and talk about stuff... like the topics found in this book.

We had some great Saturday breakfasts together, so much so that I ended up doing the same thing with our other two children during their senior years. In all three of their lives, the end result was the same. Each left home better prepared and with greater confidence for what lay ahead. And we as parents felt better about letting them go!

Over the years since then I have often been asked to put into print something that could help other kids make sure they're ready to leave home and live life on their own. And also something that could be used to open conversations between parents and their kids during those last years at home. *Just One More Thing* has been written to help do both.

If you're a student who will be leaving home within the next couple years, whether that's to go to college or just out into the world on your own, this book can help you make sure you're prepared before you go. And there are a number of different ways you could use it.

I realize that not everyone has a parent or parents that they would actually want to sit around and talk to about stuff. But if you do, it would be awesome for you to ask them to go through this book with you. Get them to take you out to breakfasts or dinners to discuss the chapters! Take the opportunity to find out more about their lives when they were your age and just heading out on their own. Once you leave home your relationship will change to a different level. They'll always be your parents, but they'll also become your friends. While you're still at home, take the time to learn from them. Give them the chance to share *just one more thing…*

There are any number of reasons why you may be in a situation where you don't have a parent or parents to go through this book with you. If that's the case, I'd encourage you to approach *Just One More Thing* like I read through Proverbs when I was your age. Allow what is written here to inform and encourage you. Read a chapter a day if you want. But take enough time to answer the refection questions found at the end of each chapter. Open your heart to what the Lord wants you to learn. Let it soak in and if necessary change you. Pray that God would help you get the most out of what you read here, so that you will be better prepared for life on your own. (And then when you're done, you might start working your way through Proverbs!) You can still profit greatly by reading *Just One More Thing* alone.

Another option is to find someone else, or a group of people, to go through this book with you. It might be a grandparent or a mentor from your church. Or maybe simply a group of your high school friends. But it could be helpful—and more fun—to work through these topics with some others.

However you choose to use *Just One More Thing*, my hope for you is the same as it was for my three children. May these topics be *just one more thing* to help you be ready for a great life out on your own after you leave home.

A NOTE TO PARENTS: This book is meant to be a tool to open up conversations between you and your child who is about to leave home. If it works for you to go through it with your son or daughter, here are some things to keep in mind:

- ❖ Please make sure you don't turn it into a series of lectures. Use this as an opportunity to simply have conversations with your child about the topics. And conversations involve not only talking but also listening.

- ❖ Be honest with them about what it was like for you when you first left home. What things weren't you prepared for? What mistakes did you make? What things do you wish you had known then? What life lessons did you learn quickly after you left home?

- ❖ Don't force them to go through this book with you. Encourage… yes. Bribe… yes. But if it becomes a battle, it's not worth it.

- ❖ And on the same note—don't make them get up at 7am on Saturday to go have breakfast with you. Figure out a time that they will be okay with. Our Saturday breakfasts were actually more of a brunch. Saturday mornings without early soccer games were sleep in days at our house!

- ❖ As you prepare for your child to leave home, remind yourself that though life will be different after they leave, your relationship will continue on in a new and exciting level. So don't feel like you have to make sure they get it all right now. This isn't your last chance to influence their lives. It's just another opportunity.

And also remember that God knew what He was doing when He put your child into your family. None of us are perfect parents. And most of us have tried our best to prepare our kids for life. Now it's time to trust God to continue leading your son or daughter in the direction He has planned for them. Never forget that He loves them even more than you do!

PART ONE

YOU
CHOOSE

one

Choices

The ball is in your court

NO ONE IN the Gudgel family will ever forget the night before our oldest son left home for college. Unfortunately that evening is indelibly stamped into everyone's minds thanks to my insistence on a mandatory Gudgel Family Meeting. It's become one of those family memories that we all laugh about now, but we weren't laughing then.

"Okay everyone," I announced, "Tonight after we have dinner, I'd like all five of us to get together in the family room for a family meeting with Brent before he leaves home tomorrow for college."

My kids aren't dumb. They intuitively knew this meeting had disaster written all over it. The likelihood that this non-optional family time would turn into an emotional nightmare was extremely high.

"Oh dad, do we have to?" Brent said. "After all, it's not our last supper together. I'd rather not have a family meeting tonight. Please, can't I just quietly leave home without making such a big deal out of it?"

"Yeah dad," our second son Brian chimed in. "It's not like we're never going to see Brent again. I mean, he's just moving into a dorm room that's only an hour away. He'll still come home again—like for Thanksgiving and Christmas."

"Well yeah, of course he'll still be around," I replied, "but from tomorrow on, Brent will officially be on his own. He'll be 'free at last' and thanking God for it! Starting tomorrow, when it comes to what Brent does and doesn't do, it'll be his choice. So before he moves out, I'd like all of us as a family to at least pray for Brent before he leaves home."

"Okay dad," Brian said, "but can we make this quick?"

That night we had "the meeting." If we had only prayed together that night for Brent, the meeting would probably have turned out okay. But instead I decided to add a time of remembering and affirmation. So as we all sat in the family room together, I asked each person to share a fun memory they had about Brent growing up and then to tell Brent one thing they will miss the most now that he would be leaving home.

I should have listened to my kids. They were right. Our final family time with Brent turned into an emotional meltdown. Everyone was crying. And I was the worst of all! (Bernice told me later that she thought I was going to have a heart attack!) It was terrible. No one left the room with a smile on their face.

After the meeting, my two other children, Brian and Katie, immediately said, "Dad, when we leave home, please please please" (from my knowledge of the Bible I knew that when a word is repeated three times in a row it is really really really important), "Don't ever do what you just did to Brent to us. That was awful. We can't go through something like that again. When it's time for each of us to leave home, let's all just write notes to each other!"

"Okay," I willingly agreed, "but I just want you to know, when you leave home it's a big deal. We're going to miss you!"

4

This Is a Big One

If you're about ready to leave home, whether to go off to college or simply to move out and live on your own, this transition is huge. For you and for your family. It's a very significant time in your life. I'm sure you know that! You're approaching one of the most important transitions you will ever face.

This change may not happen all at once, but it is one of the final steps from:

Dependence to Independence
and from
Youth to Adulthood

Your complete freedom to choose what you will or will not do on a day-to-day basis is just around the corner. You'll get to choose...

When you go to bed
When you get out of bed
If you'll make your bed
When you eat
What you eat or don't eat
If you go to college
What your major will be
When you study
The clothes you buy and wear
What friends you hang around with
If you go to church
Where you go to church
If you do or don't drink alcohol
Where you'll work

You name it, the choices will be yours to make. But what you choose to do, or not do, will definitely determine the life you live and the person you become. I agree with former UCLA basketball coach John Wooden who said, "In life you make choices, and your choices make you." Every choice you make will impact your life. You will become what you choose.

Up to this point in time, if your parents have been like Bernice and me, they have been waiting, working, and praying for the day when you're out on your own. Fully responsible for your choices and fully prepared to make good choices. But this day hasn't come overnight; it's the result of a deliberate attempt on our part as parents to decrease our authority in your life while increasing your responsibility. No doubt you, like every other child and parent, have found this year after year process challenging. But the goal has been clear. We have been trying our best to prepare you to make wise choices. This slow transitional process has taken us through three parenting stages:

STAGE ONE: PARENTS' CHOICE

In this stage we made the decisions for you. Our choice prevailed when it came to matters like when you went to bed, what you wore, what you ate, etc.

STAGE TWO: OUR CHOICE

Here we made the decisions with you. We wanted you to share in the decision-making so you would learn to make good choices on your own.

STAGE THREE: YOUR CHOICE

Here we want you to make decisions without us. And hopefully they'll be good ones! But, even the bad ones will help teach you how to make better choices in the future. What you chose to do or not do will be up to you.

The goal of this three-fold process was simple—to prepare you to make healthy responsible choices that will ultimately honor God, demonstrate love to others, and be good for you in the end.

In sports, when "the ball is in your court" it means it's your turn to play. The next step is up to you. What you do with the ball is your choice. If you're playing basketball, your goal is to get the ball through the hoop. To score two or three points. To play within the rules and defeat your opponent. You've worked hard to get the ball, now make your possession of it count.

If you're playing tennis and "the ball is in your court" it's your turn to serve or return the ball. Will you serve it low and hard or with topspin and slice? Will you smash your return or instead hit a dinky soft lob? It's your choice, and the outcome will be directly connected to what you choose to do with the ball.

Leaving home is like having your parents hand you a ball and say, "Okay, from now on what you choose to do or not do is up to you. We've done all we can to prepare you for this transition. So now it's your turn. We can hardly wait to see how you're going to play the game of life from here. If you need some help or advice, we're around. But...the ball is in your court."

The ball is in your court

Life is full of choices. Some of the choices you face will be simple (what to eat). Other choices will be hard (do I want to get into a serious relationship right now?). Some choices will be huge (what do I want to do with my life?).

How can the following verses help you with the choices you'll face in the future?

> *Joshua 24:15 – "But if serving the LORD seems undesirable to you, then choose for yourselves this day whom you will serve, whether the gods your forefathers served beyond the River, or the gods of the Amorites, in whose land you are living. But as for me and my household, we will serve the LORD."*

> *1 Corinthians 10:31 – So whether you eat or drink or whatever you do, do it all for the glory of God.*

> *Hebrews 11:24-25 – By faith Moses, when he had grown up, refused to be known as the son of Pharaoh's daughter. He chose to be mistreated along with the people of God rather than to enjoy the pleasures of sin for a short time.*

> *1 Peter 2:16 – Live as free men, but do not use your freedom as a cover-up for evil; live as servants of God.*

How prepared do you feel you are for making wise choices?

two

Advice

Frequently too much but never enough

IT TOOK AN "F" followed by a "D" to convince me I needed someone's advice. Wise counsel. Fast. Really fast. Before I failed out of Westmont College.

I transferred into Westmont as a junior having already completed my first two years of college at Fresno City College. I would love to have gone straight from high school into a four-year college, but my GPA was too low and the only college I could get into was a city college.

Looking back, being forced to enroll in a city college was perfect for me. For one, it gave me the chance to get my grades up to an acceptable GPA level that would get me into a four-year college. It also gave me time to sort out what I really wanted to do with my life and what that would mean in terms of a college major. Plus an added bonus—attending a city college was a lot cheaper!

I did what you may be thinking of doing after you graduate from high school. I moved out. Not because I hated my parents and wanted to live somewhere else. For me, I was just chomping at the bit to start living life on my own. So the summer between high school and college, with my parent's permission, I packed all my stuff into my car and moved to an apartment that I shared with a friend—to me, that counts for living life on your own. Although I was still living in the same city my parents were, living in my own place was a great experience for me. But it also meant I was on my own financially.

I was pretty much living from paycheck to paycheck. I had no college savings to fall back on. But somehow, by God's grace, my hourly jobs paid my bills and I was even able to begin saving for my dream of getting out of Fresno for my last two years of college.

My dream was fulfilled when I got accepted into Westmont College, a small Christian liberal arts college in Santa Barbara, California. Getting into Westmont was the fulfillment of two years of hard work. Academically, I was able to get my GPA up from 1.99 (my years of high school were filled with academic mediocrity) to a 3.25. And due to some incredible job doors that God opened for me, I was able to save enough money to afford to go there.

When I got to Westmont I was really motivated. First and foremost because I felt God had opened the door for me to go there. I didn't take that lightly so I wanted to do my best. Having graduated from Fresno City College with an A.A. degree, my general ed requirements had pretty much all been fulfilled, so I began Westmont right where I wanted to be, focusing on my chosen Sociology major.

During my first two years of college I had decided I wanted to go into some type of vocational ministry. So by the time I got to Westmont, I was really ready to get into my Sociology classes to help me begin preparing for whatever future ministry God opened up for me. I was also really excited about the Bible classes I would be taking there. Since I had grown up in church and had been involved the previous two years in youth ministry, I was sure I'd just sail right through those classes.

Bernice, my girlfriend from Fresno, got into Westmont at the same time I did. She however was able to do so as a freshman because she was a much better student than I was in high school. She graduated 'Summa Cum Laude' while I was 'Oh Laude Help Me Graduate!'

Both of us starting Westmont at the same time worked out to my advantage because I was able to take a few of the required Bible classes with Bernice. Our first class together was Old Testament Survey. For the first three weeks I loved that class.

Three times a week I looked forward to sitting under the brilliant teaching of Dr. Blankenbaker. I could just feel my mind expanding as I listened to his lectures. This is what college was all about! I was even looking forward to our first test.

I figured with my biblical knowledge, and study sessions with Bernice, getting an "A" in Old Testament Survey would be a breeze. My theory was put into action for our first test. We spent a lot of time going over our notes and studying together. Then the day came for the test. Two days later the scores were posted on Dr. Blankenbaker's door.

My parents taught me to let girls go first, so we looked for Bernice's score on the list of 100 students. There it was—an A. Hugs and smiles. I remember thinking, "Cool, she aced this exam…we studied together… so I must have too."

Next we looked for my score. There it was—an F. Yep—an F.

"You're kidding. No way. This has got to be a mistake!" I was in shock. And embarrassed! My girlfriend who was just a freshman got an A. while I, a junior, GOT AN F! It was terrible. Bernice felt so bad she even started to cry. Then I almost cried.

My next test opportunity came a week later in "Intro to Sociology" (thankfully, Bernice wasn't in this class!). It's the "Intro" class so it's the easy one, right? I was pumped up. I was ready for this test. I had studied all week for it. I loved the class. I loved the reading. I knew for sure this time my test results would be different.

They were. I got a D.

That's when reality hit. I can remember thinking, "I need help. BIG help. After all I did to get here, if I don't get help fast, I'm going to flunk out of Westmont and end up going back to Fresno."

So I ended up in the Dean's office. This time at my own initiative, not like the time in high school when I had no choice (but that's another story).

I sat down and blurted out, "I've taken two tests so far. I got an F and a D. If I keep this up, I'm going to flunk out. I really want to be here. I worked hard to get here. And I thought I was ready. I don't know what I'm doing wrong! I need help. Am I just not smart enough to be here?"

That day my short hour in Dean Jones office changed me academically. I will never forget it. He gave me some practical tools to use that not only helped me survive (and even excel) during my two years at Westmont; they continue to help me to this day. I learned how to take notes and keep up on my homework better. My study habits improved. My usage of time improved. And over time I learned how to take a test. When I think about the B.A degree I earned at Westmont, followed by an M.Div at Talbot Seminary, and then a D.Min at Western Seminary, I know I would have never gone that far if I hadn't willingly sought the advice and help of the Dean of Students at Westmont College and then implemented his wise counsel into my life.

When I walked into his office that day, I learned the importance of humbling myself and seeking help and advice. Since that day I've sought out the advice and counsel of others many many times. To this day I know I need others' wise and godly counsel to keep from failing or making stupid mistakes.

I've found that one of the best things you can do with the freedom you have as an independent adult, is to choose to get and keep getting advice from others. The ultimate choice (and responsibility) will still be yours, but you'll have a lot better chance of success if you seek the advice and counsel of others.

Frequently too much but never enough

Knowing that you don't know it all is a good thing. It opens you up to wanting and seeking out wise counsel.

What do the following Scriptures teach about who to seek counsel from and why?

Proverbs 19:20 – Listen to advice and accept instruction, and in the end you will be wise.

Proverbs 12:15 – The way of a fool seems right to him, but a wise man listens to advice.

Proverbs 15:22 – Plans fail for lack of counsel, but with many advisers they succeed.

Proverbs 24:6 – For waging war you need guidance, and for victory many advisers.

Psalms 119:24 – Your statutes are my delight; they are my counselors.

Proverbs 23:22 – Listen to your father, who gave you life, and do not despise your mother when she is old.

What does the following verse teach you about the frequency of asking for advice?

Proverbs 20:18 – Make plans by seeking advice; if you wage war, obtain guidance.

How do you feel about seeking future advice from your parents?

three

Convictions
Building your worldview

SOON AFTER ARRIVING at Westmont College I found that among the students, the churches of choice on any given Sunday morning were "Bedside Baptist" and "Church of the Inner Spring." I knew this was the case because I was one of the few that got out of bed to go to a Sunday morning worship service anywhere. I had to, it was my job.

Within the first week after starting college at Westmont I hustled down to the on-campus employment office to look for a job. With a personal bank balance barely above zero, I desperately needed a job in order to buy the textbooks I would be assigned, the deodorant I would need, and the spending money I would want. I was fortunate. I ended up landing two jobs.

Since Westmont is a Christian college, all students were required to attend chapel services three times a week. This miniature worship service was usually sandwiched somewhere between our morning classes. Everyone had to go to chapel, regardless of whether or not they liked the music or the speaker. Chapel was required. Attendance was taken. You didn't dare miss more than the allowed number of absences or you'd have to deal with the repercussions that began with a special invitation to meet Dean Jones in his office. It went downhill from there.

In my two years at Westmont I never missed a chapel service. I made them all. Perfect attendance. I had to be there.

I was the guy at Chapel that mastered the art of feedback. Yes, I can remember on more than one occasion having everyone turn around and stare at me like I had no clue what I was doing. Which was true. The training for my job running the Chapel PA system pretty much began and ended with the words, "Here's the on/off switch and the volume control."

Skilled or unskilled, it didn't really matter to me. I was just glad to be getting paid for going to Chapel, which I had to be at anyway. How cool was that! Besides filling out my mandatory Chapel attendance card, I also added the hours onto my time card which made me feel really good on the 1st and 15th of every month.

I also never missed going to church on Sundays. Remember—I had to. I was the guy that got paid to drive one of the school vans carrying mostly girls who didn't have their own cars to church on Sunday mornings. Going to church…with girls…and getting paid! Nice.

Westmont is in the middle of a residential neighborhood so they had to restrict the number of cars allowed on campus. That basically meant that almost all the freshman and sophomore students didn't have cars. They were forced to depend on friends who were juniors or seniors, or get rides to and from the campus on one of the Westmont shuttle buses.

Fortunately for me, before coming to Westmont I had acquired my 2nd Class Drivers license during my two years as a youth pastor. It allowed me to drive kids around in 15 passenger vans or even buses. This made me the perfect candidate to be paid to drive one of the Westmont vans.

Every Sunday vans were used to take students to church. The number and size of vans needed was based on the number of students who chose to go. Usually that meant three small vans that would drop off mostly girls at various churches of their choice. I rarely drove a guy to church because they either had their own car or just didn't go.

So, during my last two years of college I was paid to go to Chapel and to go to church. Three weekdays a week and then again on Sunday! Perfect jobs.

Besides the fact that when you leave home you also may want to look for a job that pays you to do something that you were already going to do anyway, this story raises a relevant question. In fact you may already be asking it. If I hadn't been paid to drive that van, would I have been among the 'Bedside' and 'Inner Spring' church crowd who chose to sleep in and skip church on Sunday mornings? If I wasn't being paid to run the sound system, would I have simply gone to the minimum number of required chapels?

That's a fair and important question because the answer would reveal if church or chapel attendance was merely a preference or truly a conviction for me. There's a big difference between the two.

If I have a conviction about something, it's non-negotiable. I am going to do it, or not do it, no matter what. Because I believe it's important and I'm choosing to do it, or not do it.

So if I have a conviction with regard to church, it means that going to church on Sundays is a non-negotiable. Corporately worshiping God every week is a priority in my schedule. I will do whatever it takes to get out of bed, or drop whatever else I am doing, and make time to worship with other believers.

If, on the other hand, worship is just a preference, it means I can take it or leave it. It's nice when it happens. When it's convenient. When I feel like it. When it works out. It's a good idea, but if it doesn't happen, no big deal.

Here are a few phrases that capture the difference between a conviction and a preference.

A Conviction	A Preference
I know	I think
I must	I could
I have to	I would like to
I will	I want to
I am convinced	I am uncertain

The prophet Daniel exemplified his own deeply held conviction when King Nebuchadnezzar ordered him, in preparation for service in the king's palace, to be given royal food and wine. Who wouldn't want that, right? Daniel didn't—which was pretty incredible.

When Daniel said no to the king's food and drink, he was around 15 years old and living in Babylon—far away from his parents' home in Jerusalem. Daniel was among a group of Israelites that had been taken captive by the Babylonians. He was then selected by the king, along with some other young men his age, to be given three years of training to become a personal servant to the king.

All of these young men were to be given the same preparation. They were to be taught the language and literature of the Babylonians. They were to be given new names. They were to be fed a certain diet (Daniel 1:4-6).

Daniel drew the line on what he would or would not eat. He said no to what the king wanted him to eat because he knew it had been sacrificed to idols, which was against the Jewish dietary laws. Eating that meat in Daniel's mind would be equal to participating in idol worship which was something he would not do.

But Daniel made up his mind that he would not defile himself with the king's choice food or with the wine which he drank; so he sought permission from the commander of the officials that he might not defile himself. (Daniel 1:8, NASB)

Regardless of the potential consequences from the king, or the acceptance of this diet on the part of the other young men in the crowd, Daniel said no. He asked for permission to eat vegetables and water instead.

Daniel's daring request would not have happened had he not already made up his mind not to defile himself with food that had been sacrificed to idols. He stood on what, for him, was a deeply held conviction. To the other young men, following the dietary laws was simply a preference that could be set aside when the situation warranted.

Some years ago I heard Josh McDowell say that when it comes to what students do or don't do: 75% is based on feelings, 20% on beliefs, and 5% on convictions. Personally I believe this is in part why 50 to 80% of high school students who have been raised in a church walk away from any kind of involvement in church during their first year in college. For many, church involvement was nothing more than a preference. It never became a personally chosen conviction.

When I got into college, I couldn't imagine not worshiping God on a regular basis. The fact is, during my two years at City College in Fresno I had already established the priority of regular worship in my life. The importance of it was and still is a deep personal conviction with me. So by the time I got to Westmont, I looked forward to going to church on Sundays, and attending Chapel during the week, every time it happened. Even if I wasn't getting paid, I would have been there.

I'd urge you like Daniel to determine your non-negotiable convictions before you leave home. I can assure you they will be put to the test and reveal whether something is an uncompromising conviction or simply a preference that may change depending on the circumstances at the time.

.

Building your worldview

It's been said, "A preference is something you hold, but a conviction is something that holds you."

Are convictions really that important?

Romans 14:22 – The faith which you have, have as your own conviction before God. Happy is he who does not condemn himself in what he approves.

Hebrews 11:1 – Now faith is the assurance of things hoped for, the conviction of things not seen.

Do you have a conviction or preference for the following?

Behavior or Activity	Conviction	Preference
Going regularly to a church		
Only dating believers		
Only marrying a believer		
Sexual purity before marriage		
Regular Bible reading and prayer		
Using your spiritual gifts to serve others		
Not using bad language		
Not getting drunk		
Not viewing pornography		
Avoiding impure movies or television shows		
Serving the poor		

Can you see areas where you need lines of conviction?

PART TWO

RELATIONAL INTELLIGENCE

four

Roommates
Hard to live with or without

IT NEVER OCCURRED to me before I moved out of my parents' house that living with a roommate might not be as easy or as fun as it sounded. I can still vividly remember the day I loaded all my worldly goods into my little car, waved goodbye to my parents, and drove off into the sunset. The only things on my mind were freedom & fun. I had been waiting for this day for the previous two years. Graduating from High School and turning eighteen—the two conditions my parents set before they'd let me move out—had finally been met. Living happily ever after was next for me!

At eighteen years and five days old, I thought I was ready for life on my own. Well almost on my own—I had to live with a roommate since I couldn't afford my own place. In looking back, I think that was probably the only reason my parents actually agreed to let me move out. Because I'd be living with Tim.

When Tim, the oldest—and only—friend I had who was living on his own called me one day and said he had an opening at his apartment and was wondering if I'd be interested in moving in and sharing the rent, my parents were in complete agreement with me moving out. Tim was 24-years old, didn't do drugs, didn't drink or party, and was known around our church as a really nice guy with a stable life and a full time job. My parent's prayers had been answered.

I needed Tim. But aside from my share of the rent, I'm not sure he needed me. He had everything I didn't—furniture, dishes, wisdom, a vacuum cleaner, a nice stereo, a TV, and a food filled refrigerator. During the time I lived with him, he taught me a lot about roommate survival. And since I didn't want to get kicked out, which would mean moving back home, I was more than willing to learn from him.

"Dave, when you use dishes, please wash them right after you use them and put them away. I don't like dirty dishes in the sink."

"Well okay, sure, whatever you want Tim."

"And the food in the refrigerator on the top three shelves is mine. Please don't eat it. You can keep your food on the bottom two shelves."

"Got it. No problem. I don't like bologna and broccoli anyway."

"And Dave, I'll dust the furniture once a week on Saturday. Since I'm doing the dusting, would you mind doing the vacuuming?"

Dude, I thought, I'd rather not. I'd rather go with the "vacuum only when you can no longer tell what color the carpet is" plan. But somehow I knew make-your-bed-every-day Tim wouldn't go for that. So I simply said...

"Sure Tim, I love to vacuum. Used to watch my mom do it all the time."

"And Dave, I hate cleaning toilets. It makes me gag. So I hope you're okay with keeping that clean? The toilet bowl cleaner's under the sink."

That's when I almost lost it. If you look at me closely you can still see the scar from where I bit my lip. I faked a smile and forced myself to say, "Sure Tim. Anything for you. I'm just glad to be able to live here" (and have my mom close by who loves me and has done toilets for about 100 years).

Rude awakening. So much for life finally being one big party. Instead, my parents' expectation list was being replaced with an even more demanding list. Sheesh, at least my mom cleaned the toilets! But I wasn't stupid and I knew that this time my compliance could mean the difference between living free at last or being forced to move back home.

I realize now that my feelings, though unexpected to me, were very common. Pretty much everyone else who's ever lived with another person has faced the same thing I faced. I've come to call it the Expectation Gap. I picture it this way:

Your Roommate's Expectations

> ### The
> ### Expectation
> ### GAP

Your Expectations

Here's the deal—which often is a deal breaker. The bigger the gap between your expectations and your roommate's expectations, the bigger the potential for disappointment, frustration, anger, disagreement, and even feelings of depression.

After I moved away from home, over the next four years I lived with four different roommates. First Tim, then Sam, then John, then Marty. One was a roommate for three months. Another for a record breaking eighteen months. And I lived with each of the other two for about a year.

My roommate experience was similar to many of my friends, and actually for all three of my kids too. Educational. Life changing. Challenging. Fun at times. Horrible at others. Usually short-term, which was often due to a huge gap between my expectations and my roommate's.

Living with a roommate can have a ton of advantages. First on the list is the financial benefit, followed by friendship and fun. But perhaps the best advantage of all is the relational benefit gained when things don't turn out like you planned (though you probably won't think that at the time!). When you start thinking you'd rather be living with someone else. When you find out that what you originally saw about your then soon-to-be roommate on Facebook, that you really liked, didn't tell the whole story. Now you find this person you thought could be a close friend is really someone who's hard to get along with. Someone you'd rather not spend time with. Someone who annoys you...a lot. You've found yourself counting the days until one of you moves out. One thing is for sure—when you move to another dorm next year, you're going to live with someone else—and start all over again…

Don't get me wrong, most kids who move away from home are ready to live with a roommate, whether it's in a college dorm or in an apartment, in exchange for the freedom and fun it can give. It can be worth it and truly a lot of fun. But before you move out of your parents' home and into a new home with someone else, you'll do yourself a big favor if you make a few pre-roommate harmony commitments, which are at the forefront of Paul's thoughts in Philippians 2:2-4 where he says:

> *Make my joy complete by being like-minded, having the same love, being one in spirit and purpose. Do nothing out of selfish ambition or vain conceit, but in humility consider others better than yourselves. Each of you should look not only to your own interests, but also to the interests of others.*

Paul has the same thing in mind that you should when you move in with someone—the desire to live together in harmony and love. Able to get along with each other. Aligned in purpose and direction. Enjoying peace. You want this to be a really good experience. Paul says that living with this kind of joy is possible of you will make three commitments.

SWALLOW YOUR PRIDE

It's not an accident that the first thing on Paul's relational harmony list is humility, which is the opposite of pride. Pride builds walls, humility builds bridges. Pride is full of selfishness and ego. It boasts that its way is the best way. It shouts "do it my way." It thinks, "I'm right. I know better."

Humility, on the other hand, focuses on serving others, rather than getting them to serve you. It's not found in thinking less of yourself, but it's the result of thinking of yourself less. It asks, "How can I help? How can we make things right? What can we do to make things better?"

VALUE YOUR ROOMMATE

Every time we have a relationship with another person, it's as if we all have an invisible sign hanging around our necks that asks, "Do I matter to you?" I wear one. You wear one. And your future roommates will all wear them. How you treat your roommates will determine if they feel like they matter to you.

If you follow Paul's advice and *"consider others as better than yourself,"* your roommate will feel better, not worse, when they are with you. He or she will feel inspired, valued, and respected rather than demeaned and belittled.

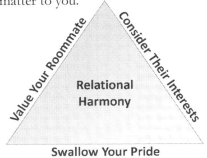

Pastor Chuck Swindoll tells the story of a time when, in the middle of playing a racquetball game with one of his associate pastors, Chuck asked, "What are you all about?" Without even a moment of thought, this other pastor replied, "Making you great, Chuck."

I can make you a guarantee—if you adopt that same attitude toward your roommate, your roommate is going to love you and you're going to love living on your own.

CONSIDER THEIR INTERESTS

Paul's final piece of advice for living with relational harmony is like something you did in biology when you *scoped something out* through a microscope. Paul writes that we are to *skopeō* closely each other's interests. That means to pay close attention to others' likes and dislikes. Become a student of their preferences. Make note of what they like and what annoys them. Then make relational adjustments that take their interests into account.

For example, let's say you have a roommate who likes to go to bed early, and you don't. Out of consideration for their "early to bed, early to rise" schedule, if you're in the room or come into the room after they've gone to bed, be quiet. Don't bang things around. Use a dim light. Do your best to not annoy them. Hopefully they'll do the same for you in the morning when they're getting up while you're still trying to sleep!

Thank God For Roommates

Marty, my last roommate, was different. By that I mean different from me. First of all because he was smart. I mean really smart. He graduated at the top of our class and went on to become a pediatrician. He was messy. I was organized. He liked to go to bed late. I liked to go to bed early. He was quiet. I was loud. He hardly ever said a thing. I hardly ever stopped talking.

But in spite of all our differences, we really got along well and probably would have lived as roommates again had we not gone our separate ways after college graduation. He went on to med school. I started working full-time and eight months later got married and began the ultimate living together experience that has lasted now for more than thirty years. In today's world, that would be considered a success, which I believe is due in part to the invaluable lessons learned from the life-changing years I lived with four different roommates.

Hard to live with or without

Now is a great time to start getting yourself ready for living with a roommate. Here are a few questions that will begin to prepare you for what I hope will be one of the best times of your life.

What are your top five expectations that you have for a future roommate?

1. _____
2. _____
3. _____
4. _____
5. _____

How will the following three commitments help you and your roommate live in harmony?

- A commitment to "Swallow your pride"

- A commitment to "Value your roommate"

- A commitment to "Consider their interests"

What will you do if your roommate doesn't meet all of your expectations and doesn't share these three commitments?

five

Authenticity
Deal with the elephant in the room

AS YOU PREPARE to move out on your own, you might as well accept the fact right up front that none of us are perfect. We all have issues. Agreed? Which means there are no perfect relationships either. And in every relationship, things are going to come up that can become the elephant in the room that everyone knows is there but no one wants to talk about.

Trust me, living with a roommate *plus* an elephant in the room is not fun. That's how I lived for the first three months of my college dorm experience— me, Sam, and an elephant in the room. That continued until I finally couldn't take it anymore and moved out.

For those three months, Sam and I faked it. We acted like everything in our roommate relationship was fine when it wasn't. Yet neither of us took the necessary steps to fix what ultimately led to us parting company.

Looking back, I now realize the problem wasn't a big issue, it was a bunch of little things. But instead of talking about the stuff in healthy ways, I tip-toed around it all and pretended it wasn't there. Things weren't fine, even though I acted like they were whenever

Sam asked how I was doing.

So what were the little things? Well, for one, I hated the fact that Sam was a slob. Nobody would have guessed it. Outside our dorm room, Sam, in his carefully purchased, deliberately picked, and perfectly worn clothes looked great. But inside our dorm room, his unwashed, smelly, designer clothes were thrown all over his side of the room that was still way too close to where I slept.

Could I have said something? Sure. Did I? No. What was I thinking? Haven't got a clue. Maybe it was my man genes that kept me from saying something about his dirty jeans. The ones that whispered inside my head, "Suck it up and be a man about this. What kind of sissy are you anyway? Are you going to let a pile of dirty clothes bother you? Get used to it."

Or maybe it was the stubborn streak in me that said, "I shouldn't *have* to say anything about this. He should know better. Didn't his mom teach him to clean up after himself?!"

And there were other things that bugged me too. Like our differences about music, schedules, noise levels during study times, half-eaten food all over the room… Well you get the idea.

But did I say anything to Sam about any of this? No. I just kind of hoped that he'd figure it out on his own and decide to change. And since I'm not that good of an actor, it was obvious to both of us that there was a problem. That there was a big elephant in the room.

We went on that way for four months. For one hundred and twenty days Sam and I lived with that stupid elephant. And then we parted company. Sam stayed in that dorm room and I moved out for a new life in a new dorm with a new roommate. And I hoped the elephant wouldn't come with me!

I can't say our undoing was all Sam's fault. I'm sure if he were writing this story he'd have a few things to say about *my* issues that annoyed *him*. But the bottom line is the same—it's really really hard for relationships to survive when there's an elephant hanging around that everyone pretends isn't there.

If You Care, Share

God's Word has a lot to say about this. Want God's best for yourself and others? "Speak the truth in love" (Ephesians 4:15,25). Want to work things out instead of moving out? Don't forget the proverb that teaches, "Faithful are the wounds of a friend; but deceitful are the kisses of an enemy" (Proverbs 27:6, NASB).

Acting like nothing is wrong when something is wrong, is something an enemy would do, not a friend. If you really care, lovingly share the truth. Even if it's going to be hard for them to hear. If you really care, share! Because when you do, the process toward a better future is started.

That's why David, who knew the value of this kind of friendship, said, "Let the godly strike me! It will be a kindness! If they correct me, it is soothing medicine. Don't let me refuse it" (Psa 141:5a, MSG). In other words, if you see something in me that needs correction, you have my full permission to give me what I need. Slap me where I need to be slapped. Even if it's painful, I need you to come along and help me heal. I can't do this without you. And if I refuse to swallow the medicine you're giving me, don't give up on me. Stick with me until I get it. Because I need to get it if I am ever going to get well. In the end, what may seem unkind will be exactly what I need.

You In Four Parts

Some years ago I was introduced to the Johari window. A chart of windowpanes that describes four areas in our lives:

OPEN	BLIND
I See	I Don't See
Others See	Others See
HIDDEN	**UNKNOWN**
I See	I Don't See
Others Don't See	Others Don't See

The Johari window, created in 1969 by Joseph Luft and Harry Ingham, can be a helpful tool in understanding yourself and others. Simply stated, our lives are made up of four areas:

- Our **open** self: all the things about us that we see and others also see.

- The **hidden** self: the things about me that I see but you can't because I'm hiding that part of my life from you.

- The **unknown** self: the parts of my life that neither of us see.

- The **blind** self: the parts of my life that you see, but I don't.

Not Just What But How

I can still remember the day when I sat down with a friend who needed to hear the truth about an area of his life that was holding him back from becoming all he could be. I had determined in my heart to "speak the truth." To help him see his blind spot. To give him some soothing medicine. The only problem was, I conveniently disregarded the "in love" part of speaking the truth.

It wasn't so much what I said that was the problem, but how I said it. After several minutes of listening to me rant on about the stupidity of something my friend had done, I paused to see what his reply would be. In my stupidity, I expected him to say something like, "Oh Dave, you are so right. I blew it. I can't believe I was so stupid. I really don't know what I was thinking. Thank you soooo much for having the courage to confront me about this."

Was that his response? Not even close. Instead he said, "Dave, you're right. I did blow it. I could have done better. And I hope to do better in the future, but…" In looking back, this ended up being one of the moments in my life when I seriously needed to pay attention to the "but" because what followed changed me.

"But…" he said, "how you shared with me what you just shared with me was wrong. I may be wrong, but you are too. At least in how you've said what you just said to me. You were condescending and demeaning. I agree I *did* something stupid, but you spoke to me like you think *I'm* stupid. If you ask me, that is just as wrong as the wrong I have done."

Touché. That hurt. But it needed to hurt because in my desire to help I had hurt my friend deeply by the way I spoke to him. I learned an important lesson that day about speaking the truth *in love*.

More Than Words
Several years ago Albert Mehrabian found that communication involves a lot more than just words. His studies showed that words only account for 7% of what is communicated. The other 93% comes from our tone of voice (38%) and body language (55%).

A lot of what we communicate to others is done through non-verbal means. Even when you aren't saying anything, you are saying something. And when you speak, how you say what you say could scream a lack of love even if it's said with a soft tone of voice.

Communicating with each other in authentic and yet loving ways is a lifelong challenge. Some of us have personalities that make truth telling easier, but the "saying it in love" part can be a struggle. While others may find it's easy to say things in a loving way, but find it hard to actually get up the nerve to speak the truth.

Whichever side of that you fall into, hopefully you'll work at finding a balance between the two. We'll all be better off if we learn to speak the truth in love instead of simply bailing on a relationship and moving on to someone new—until an elephant shows up in that relationship too!

Do you remember the story of the emperor who wasn't wearing any clothes? The poor guy was unknowingly running around buck naked and no one said anything because it wasn't their place to speak up. But then finally a kid came along and said what everyone else had been thinking, "The emperor has no clothes!" The emperor needed that little boy's honesty!

When there are issues causing strain and friction in a relationship, pretending everything's fine won't work for long. Eventually even something little can become a giant elephant in the room. And if you're not willing to face the problem head on, the relationship is most likely headed for failure. The best thing you can do to maintain the relationship, and even make it stronger, is to lovingly speak the truth..

Deal with the elephant in the room

The next time you are in a situation where you need to "speak the truth in love." how can the following verses help you say the right words in the right way?

> *Ephesians 4:25 – Therefore each of you must put off falsehood and speak truthfully to his neighbor, for we are all members of one body.*

> *Proverbs 27:6 – Wounds from a friend can be trusted, but an enemy multiplies kisses.*

> *Psalm 141:5a – Let a righteous man strike me--it is a kindness; let him rebuke me--it is oil on my head. My head will not refuse it.*

> *Ephesians 4:29 – Do not let any unwholesome talk come out of your mouths, but only what is helpful for building others up according to their needs, that it may benefit those who listen.*

six

Love
Looking for "the one"

I AM OF THE OPINION that a guy or girl who says they aren't looking for *the one*, actually is. Though it may just be out of the corner of their eye. That's pretty much how it happened with Caleb and Kylie. To this day, neither is sure who first noticed the other. But it happened, even though—and let me quote them on this—"Pastor Dave, we weren't looking. Really. After all, we were at church."

Really?

Had it not been for their mothers, who each independently suggested they attend a worship service at the church I pastored, they may have never met.

"Here's what I remember about my first Sunday at Bethany Bible Church," Caleb told me. "I came in and sat down on the aisle somewhere near the back. I looked around. When I glanced to the other side of the aisle—bam—this really cute girl caught my eye. After that, I pretty much didn't hear anything you said the rest of the morning."

"It was a little different for me," Kylie said. "I didn't notice Caleb until at the point in the service when everyone is encouraged to take a minute and greet each other. Well I turned around and said hi to a couple of people behind me and then noticed this really cute guy across the aisle."

The next Sunday, without their mothers' urging, they both came back to the same service and sat in the same general area. This continued for a couple months as they gradually moved toward each other chair-by-chair, row-by-row. I kid you not. Each of them, unbeknownst to the other, kept moving closer until they ended up sitting immediately in front and behind each other.

On that fateful day, they both anxiously awaited the cue from the worship leader for everyone to "turn and greet those around you." After two months of waiting, this was the moment each of these two very shy twenty-something's had waited for. Finally they would meet with more than just their eyes.

If we had given out pins for perfect attendance, Caleb and Kylie would each have deserved one. Over the next two months they didn't miss a service, nor did they fail to strategically sit near each other so they could say hi before and after the service and during the greeting.

Then our worship planning team unknowingly did Caleb and Kylie a big favor by planning a 10-minute Coffee Break right in the middle of the service. No more 30-second hand shake and hello greetings. This was a serious opportunity to actually talk to each other!

When the Coffee Break was announced, Kylie was too shy to start a conversation with Caleb so she took off for the snack table where she picked up a Mountain Dew. When she turned around, she saw Caleb talking to "a really cute girl." Wanting to kick herself for not staying and talking to Caleb during the break, she figured all her chair relocation efforts had been pointless.

But Caleb wasn't going to give up that easy. At the end of the service as Kylie was walking out of the Chapel he caught up with her and said, "Kylie, I want you to know something."

"Oh? What?"

"Well, today I wanted to spend the Coffee Break talking to you but then this girl came up and started talking to me."

"Oh…I was wondering who that cute girl was?"

"Actually, I had never met her before, and I wanted you to know that…and I was wondering if you would be interested in going out for dinner with me this coming Saturday?"

Kylie said yes. And for the next year they built a great friendship and then a very special boyfriend/girlfriend relationship. They took it slow and did what I strongly recommend couples do who have an interest in each other.

A STRONG SPIRITUAL FOUNDATION

Knowing Caleb and Kylie pretty well, I kid them about their real reasons for initially coming to church. But the fact is, each of them loves the Lord and longs to grow closer to Him. That driving personal desire led to a strong spiritual dimension in their relationship with each other, and built a strong foundation for what they are now experiencing as a husband and wife.

I tell couples all the time, strong relationships are built on a strong spiritual foundation. Your spiritual connection with God and each other is the most important connection you can make. Without a strong spiritual foundation, even your best attempts at building a relationship will fall short of what God could give you.

When it comes to homebuilding, the Bible says, "Unless the Lord builds the house, its builders labor in vain" (Psa 127:1). Simply said, you're crazy to think you can build a great home without God. You need His help. From the ground up. Otherwise your most important relationships in life are destined to crash and burn. From the start, Caleb and Kylie knew that and sought God's leading and wisdom and help in all that they did as a couple.

A GROWING EMOTIONAL CONNECTION

As Caleb and Kylie built their spiritual relationship, they also developed a growing emotional connection. Their hearts and souls were slowly knit together into a deeper and deeper friendship. Beginning with their first dinner date at the Bamboo Club, they continued to grow in their understanding of each others' thoughts and feelings. What started as an eye-to-eye relationship progressed to a mind-to-mind, heart-to-heart, and then soul-to-soul connection.

They talked for hours about each others' views and opinions. They discovered the things they were each passionate about. Many times they found themselves saying, "Wow, that's what you think about that? So do I?" Of course there were also times when they realized they saw something through a different lens, which made for some very interesting conversations.

All the while their love and respect for each other grew, as did their soul connection. They opened their hearts up to each other in ways only done with a trusted friend. They shared their innermost struggles and fears, hopes and dreams, joys and sorrows. They found themselves more and more devoted to each other in brotherly love (Rom 12:10)—the kind of love shared by close personal friends.

A CHALLENGING PHYSICAL COMMITMENT

As you can imagine, Caleb and Kylie experienced a natural sexual attraction to each other. They longed to express their love by more than just holding hands. They experienced the same feelings King Solomon did for his girlfriend.

When Solomon told their love story, three times he mentions how challenging it was to not "awaken or arouse love until it so desires" (Song of Solomon 2:7). That was a discreet way of saying, "We really wanted to have sex but we didn't because we weren't married yet." And so they did what any couple who wants the blessing of the Lord does. They waited. They held back on the physical until after they were married.

Caleb and Kylie did the same thing. It wasn't an easy commitment to keep. It never is. But they knew if they kept that commitment, God would be pleased and their spiritual and emotional relationship would grow stronger. Unhindered by the physical.

The also knew that if they did some day consider getting married, that decision wouldn't be driven by the physical, which can so easily deceive a couple into believing they have found the one when in reality they haven't. Once a couple starts having sex, their physical involvement can blind them to the truth about their relationship.

Whether you're looking for the one yet or not, it's a good idea to prepare yourself now before you get out of high school and into the years where dating and sex and marriage are very real possibilities. When you meet someone who might be "the one", the best way to figure it all out is by building a strong spiritual foundation, along with a growing emotional connection, while holding onto a godly physical commitment to wait.

Moms everywhere love Caleb and Kylie's story. "You see!" they say. "Always listen to your mother. When we encourage you to do something, do it! Good things will happen."

Oh and by the way, we still plan occasional Coffee Breaks in our worship services.

Looking for "the one"

Now is the time to figure out your relational plan of attack. Let the following verses help you set in place a plan for that day when you catch a glimpse of someone across the room.

What spiritual commitments does God want you to make?

2 Corinthians 6:14 – Do not be yoked together with unbelievers. For what do righteousness and wickedness have in common? Or what fellowship can light have with darkness?

Psalm 127:1a – Unless the LORD builds the house, its builders labor in vain.

Joshua 24:15b – "But as for me and my household, we will serve the LORD."

What emotional connection do you hope to develop?

Proverbs 18:24 – A man of many companions may come to ruin, but there is a friend who sticks closer than a brother.

1 Samuel 18:1– Now it came about when he had finished speaking to Saul, that the soul of Jonathan was knit to the soul of David, and Jonathan loved him as himself. (NASB)

What physical limits do you intend to keep?

1 Thessalonians 4:3-4 – It is God's will that you should be sanctified: that you should avoid sexual immorality; that each of you should learn to control his own body in a way that is holy and honorable.

1 Corinthians 6:18 – Flee from sexual immorality. All other sins a man commits are outside his body, but he who sins sexually sins again.

PART THREE

FINANCIAL
CHALLENGES

seven

Money
Living on a few bucks

FROM MY FIRST and second-hand college experience, I can say with certainty the overwhelming majority of college students are cash poor. I'm not saying they are poor, like in comparison to the rest of the world. The fact that a young adult is even able to go to college would suggest they are rich in comparison to the rest of the world. But the fact still remains, most college students at any given point in time are trying to live on too few bucks. I know I was.

The home I grew up in squeaked by financially. We always had food to eat and clothes to wear, but we lived from paycheck to paycheck, like so many other families.

So when I was getting ready to graduate from high school, my dad and mom said, "Dave, we really want you to go to college. And we hope you will. But we are not going to be able to help you out financially. So good luck with that!"

Actually, they didn't add the last five words. I did. In my mind. Their checkbook spoke for itself. My parents were in no position to help me out financially. If college was in my future, it would be up to God to make it possible for me to pay my way. And as I tried to figure out how all this was going to play out, I realized my life verse was about to be tested.

Needed advice about keeping God first

If you're not familiar with Matthew 6:33, I'd recommend you get intimately acquainted with the words of Jesus found there. In fact, I'd urge you to memorize them.

Speaking to a worry--filled group of people, Jesus said, "But seek first His kingdom and His righteousness, and all these things will be added to you" (Matt. 6:33 NASB). Just like us, the men and women Jesus spoke to were worried about providing for their basic needs. "How will we eat? What will we wear? Where will we live?" Ever asked questions like that? I have. Like right after my parents said, "Dave, we'd love to help you pay for college, but we can't."

With no college savings to fall back on and a GPA too low to qualify for an academic scholarship, there was no chance I could spend my freshman year at an expensive four-year college. If I was going to go to college I had one option—a two-year city college where the price was right, which meant the price was really low.

I set my sights on Fresno City College, but then found out that my paycheck from the custodial job I had would not be enough to pay for my rent, food, car insurance and gasoline, school tuition, lab fees, books, deodorant, an occasional date… You get the idea. That's when I committed Matthew 6:33 to memory and decided to seek God first in everything I did. Including when I needed more income to live on and to pay for the cheap college I was about to attend.

Are you familiar with the words "nothing is impossible with God"? He sure proved that in my cash poor life. Shortly after I started to look for a new, better paying job the Lord provided a dream part-time job at an architect's office. I say it was a dream job because I was planning on majoring in Architecture with the hopes of making that my career. So I really couldn't have asked for a better place to work. Not only did it pay me pretty well, it gave me experience that would help me with my future career path. That day job, plus my nighttime custodial job, gave me just enough money to pay for college and stay current with my bills. I didn't get rich, but I did get by. Plus it increased my faith for a bigger financial challenge that was yet to come.

In my sophomore year, as my two-year Junior College experience was coming to a close, I began to get a realistic picture of how much more expensive it was going to be for me to transfer to another college for my last two years.

Fortunately I had successfully raised my GPA during my two years in Junior College so I now actually qualified for a four-year college. That was great, but financially I was right back where I started. My two jobs were paying me enough to meet my current needs, but it wasn't enough for me to take on tuition for two years at a four-year college. If I was going to be able to finish my college education, I needed a new summer job that would pay me enough to cover the serious increase in tuition and room & board that was coming my way.

Your part, God's part

Once again, I did what I could do and trusted God to do whatever He chose to do. I prayed and sought the Lord's answer for my needs. My prayer went something like this, "Lord, I would love to finish my college education because I believe it's what you want me to do. But for me to do that, I need a new job. A better paying job. A summer job that will give me a lot of money and allow me to go on to college." That prayer became a regular part of my life in the last few months of my Junior College experience, as did filling out a lot of job applications.

I can still remember the day when after all of the prayer, and all of the unsuccessful attempts to get a job, I got down on my knees again, only this time to pray, "Lord, I have seen your blessing in my life over these past two years as you have provided for all my needs. I am so grateful. Thank you so much. But Lord, you know that for me to finish my college education, I need more money and therefore I need a better paying job. So Father, if you want me to finish my college education at Westmont, you are going to have to do what I can't—give me a new job. Lord, I think I've done all I can, so unless there is another place you want me to apply, would you please give me another job. Soon! Really soon!"

This really happened

Now what I am about to say is not a prescription for how the Lord always works, so please understand this before you read what happened. But God is my witness, what follows is a description of what He did in answer to that prayer.

Like God blessed Jabez, He blessed me beyond my wildest dreams. Two days after I got down on my knees and essentially prayed, "Lord, I've done all I can do, now it is up to You to do what I can't do," God did it.

A large lumber company where I had applied called me and said they wanted to give me a job. They asked me to come in for a final interview and to take a physical with their company doctor. As you can imagine I was ecstatic. God had answered my prayer. This great paying job was going to make it possible for me to go away to college.

I went in for the interview and physical and I was thrilled when they hired me. Before I left the lumber yard that day, the foreman handed me a new yellow helmet and said, "Welcome aboard. You start on Monday morning at 7:00am." Not only had God given me a new job, He had also given me five days of leisure before my new job began. At least that's what I thought until I got home.

Within two hours of being hired at the lumber yard, the California Department of Forestry called and offered me a summer job fighting forest fires. This was one of the other jobs I had applied for a few weeks before—without any luck. And now they finally called after I had gotten another job!

I was about to say "no thanks, I have another job," but I decided to ask how much this job would pay. I don't remember the exact amount, but it was a lot. It was more than I would make at the lumber yard. So I quickly said, "I'm interested!" Then they told me to come in the next day for a final interview and to take a physical. I kid you not! Two physicals in two days! Once again I went in the next day... and was hired. It was a little awkward when later that day I took my yellow helmet back to the lumber yard and quit before I had even worked one day.

All of that would be more than enough to make a person say, "Praise God! Thank you Lord!" But God had one more unanticipated surprise to drop on me.

The following Monday morning I received a call from Pittsburg Plate Glass (PPG). Of all the jobs I had applied for, this was the one I wanted most. At the time I knew a couple of other college friends who worked for them as summer hires. The pay was fantastic! And, once you got on one summer, you were pretty much assured that you would be working for them the following summer.

"We'd like to hire you for summer help," they said. "Are you interested? If you are, we'd like you to come down tomorrow for a final interview and to take a physical." I kid you not.

Yes, I did go down to PPG, and yes I did take another physical, and yes I did get hired, and yes I did quit my Forest Fire Fighting job before I had even worked one day. And yes, God gave me that job at PPG that summer and the following summer. And yes, as you've already heard, I did go to Westmont College and was able to pay for my financial obligations for the next two years.

Where God guides, He provides
The Lord said, "Seek first His kingdom and His righteousness, and all these things (food, clothing, housing, and even a college education) will be provided." I definitely believe those words!

It's been said, "Where God guides, God provides." If God wants you in college, and you don't have the money to pay for it, He'll provide what you need. He may not give you all you want, but He will give you all you need. What you don't have, He will add. And what He adds will be enough. Even if you only have a few bucks left over on which to live. As long as you're living in the center of God's will, seeking God's kingdom first. What could be better than that?

Living on a few bucks

Committing yourself to seek God's kingdom first is one of the best commitments you can make in life. What you can't do, God can do, if you will seek to live for Him first in all you do.

In what ways do you see a need for God to be first in your life right now?

How can you apply what Jesus taught in Matthew 6:33 to your life right now?

> *Matthew 6:33 – But seek first His kingdom and His righteousness, and all these things will be added to you.*

eight

Debt
Too much, too soon

MOST STUDENTS who graduate from college are in debt. Sometimes it's because of bad choices, but more often than not it's simply because college is expensive. And if you're not living at home with your parents... so is life!

It's possible that what you are about to read will have no bearing on your life if your last name is Gates, Jobs, Buffet, Zuckerberg, or Page. If that's the case, you're among the 14% that make it through college without needing a Federal Student Loan or a loan of another kind. Start counting your blessings, because you are among a blessed select group. And you might as well skip this chapter, unless you'd like to do something to help those who aren't as fortunate as you.

But most of us—and that would include me, my wife, and our three children—graduate from college with varying degrees of debt. 86% of those who go to college borrow money and end up with an average of around $25,000 in debt. But that's not necessarily a bad thing. College debt can be okay as long as you're careful and intentional about how much you borrow, and how you pay it back.

Mind Your Mind

Solomon was not only one of the wisest men who ever lived, but he was also one of the richest men who ever lived. In the midst of his pursuit for satisfaction he once said, "My mind still guided me with wisdom (Ecclesiastes 2:3b)." I love what he had in mind about his mind. Whatever you do, you're always better off when you stop and think about what you're doing. When you're guided by wisdom. By truth like that found in God's Word.

When it comes to money matters, the ultimate statement from God on whether you should or should not get into debt is "Owe no one anything, except to love each other, for the one who loves another has fulfilled the law" (Romans 13:8).

Taken on its own this statement could lead you to believe debt is off limits. Period. But I don't think that's what the Apostle Paul was saying because his primary point is that each of us lives with an ongoing debt to love each other. Like God loves us. And that debt will never be paid off. Love is something we will always owe each other.

We are also obligated to pay our financial debts. That's expected. And not just expected, but required. But unlike our debts of love, financial debts are only owed until they are completely repaid.

Paul isn't saying you can't have debt, but he is saying you are indebted to pay your debts. The NIV translation puts it like this, "Let no debt remain outstanding." If you have debt, pay it back. On time. That thought is key in determining if you should or should not have debt, and how much you can afford to have.

Reasonable and Payable

As I already said, if it had not been for a great summer job and student loans, I would not have been able to finish my last two years of college. My education would have ended after two years at City College. But the Lord, my hard work, and our government made it possible for me to attend and pay for my two years at Westmont.

When I started looking for a college to attend I was focusing on location and learning (In the interest of full disclosure, I guess I should include ladies there too!). I wanted to go to a school that was in a great location and that would also give me a great education.

If you know anything about Fresno, you can probably guess that *any location* other than Fresno (the place I am glad to be *from*) would have been a good location. But since I loved the beach, I wanted to attend a college on the West Coast. I realize that the East Coast also has beaches, but since I'm a California native the East Coast didn't even cross my mind.

And when I say West Coast I literally meant the coast—like Pt. Loma where the guys dorm sits on the beach. Seriously, at that school the guys can climb out their dorm window and jump down on the sand. Nice! And if I couldn't get into Pt. Loma, Pepperdine would have been okay too. Ever been there? You know all those pictures of star sightings on the beach in Malibu that the entertainment magazines post? That's where Pepperdine is located —a little piece of heaven on earth.

Well I didn't end up at either Pt. Loma or Pepperdine. Why? Money. Well actually a lack of money. For some reason colleges that close to the beach cost a lot more! But I got close. I ended up living in a beach city and attended Westmont where on a good day… if you stood on a certain rock near the library… and tilted your head a certain way… and looked between two specific trees, you could see the ocean in the distance. ahhhh

Whatever your criteria for the college of your choice, you've got to use your mind on this one and a lot of prayer. If you must go into debt, you need to carefully consider *doable debt* vs. *destructive debt*. One is manageable. The other will manage you. Destructive debt, the Bible says, makes you the slave of the lender. And that bondage can be painful and make you miserable for a very long time.

If you do go into debt, you need to make sure you know how you're going to get out of it. Preferably ASAP. And that's why you really want to be careful about any debt you get into, and therefore the college you choose to attend. You need to think through whether or not paying off this debt will be doable. You don't want to set yourself up for problems in the years ahead.

Your bottom line goal should be to attend a college that is good for you and one you can afford. Or at least that you can afford to pay off once you graduate.

You've probably heard a ton about the cost of college. Yep, it's expensive. And getting worse every year. But there are also a wide variety of colleges with a wide variety of costs. And there's always the option of attending a Junior College for your first two years where the average cost of tuition and fees may be less than $3000 a year. Even attending a 4-year state college could be less than $10,000 a year—which isn't bad when compared with a private 4-year college that usually costs in the neighborhood of $35,000 a year.

Deciding what college to attend is a huge decision that is often made based on the scholarships or loans offered. But debt considerations should be just as important. And while I am at it, if you hope to marry someday, you may even want to consider the magnitude of debt that the two of you will have, if your future spouse comes with their own accumulated debt.

Good Looking
So when you start looking for a college, keep these two things in mind related to the cost:

- How much is it going to cost?
- If I need to take out loans, will I be able to repay them?

That's the bottom line. Somebody is going to have to pay this back, and if your parents are like us, it's not going to be them.

Each one of our three children chose to go to a private Christian college. Academic scholarships helped, as did school loans. Each worked some. And then we as their parents paid as much as we could but we told them *we* weren't taking out any loans for them because we didn't want to be paying them off in our old age! So our kids all ended up with debt after they graduated. But it's doable debt. And now they're in the process of repaying it.

Minimal Debt

Here's the bottom line. If you must borrow money to go to college, try to get out of there with as small a debt as possible, so that once you're out, paying it off will be doable.

Obviously the college you choose will be a big part of making this work. But there are also other choices you'll need to be aware of. How you choose to live—and spend money—while you're in college will affect the amount you have to eventually pay off too. It can be really tempting to use that *oh so easy to get* college loan (or that *oh so easy to get* credit card!) for other things that you don't really need but that would be *oh so fun to have or do*. But those ski trips and annual passes to Disneyland add up fast. And four years' worth of all that fun stuff could easily move your debt from doable to destructive.

Let me leave you with one last suggestion for this chapter. It can be really smart to limit your loans to your major college expenses— tuition and room & board. If you can manage to work for a paycheck that will cover your day-to-day expenses and your books and all the random fun things that come along, that will help keep those loans down and more manageable once you start paying them off!

Too much, too soon

Life includes a series of endless spending opportunities that can easily put you into deep debt. Now is the time to determine the relationship you will have with debt.

How can the truth of these Scriptures guide you in deciding if you should or should not go into debt?

> *Proverbs 22:7 – The rich rule over the poor, and the borrower is servant to the lender.*
>
> *Psalm 37:21 – The wicked borrow and do not repay, but the righteous give generously;*
>
> *Romans 13:8 – Let no debt remain outstanding, except the continuing debt to love one another, for he who loves his fellowman has fulfilled the law.*

Do you think it will be necessary for you to go into debt in order to go to college? If so, write out a few guidelines that would be good for you to use in thinking through where and how much.

nine

Spending
You need food, but you want steak

BUT I REALLY WANT IT Disease. You won't find it on Wikipedia or in a medical journal, but that doesn't make it any less real. In fact, try looking up *discontent*. That pretty much describes *But I Really Want It* Disease. The restless desire for something more. Something better. Something that will satisfy. Something that will make everything better.

No one is immune to this disease. We humans all struggle with it from the day we're born. Adam blamed it on Eve. Eve blamed it on that darn snake. My son blamed it on Jimmy.

I can still remember the day our son Brent came home showing severe symptoms of *But I Really Want It* Disease. Just thirty minutes before, he'd grabbed his roller skates and left our home very content and happy, eager to cruise around the neighborhood with his friend Jimmy who lived a few houses away.

Just as Brent was gliding up to Jimmy's house on his roller skates, Jimmy flew out of his garage on his brand new—and very very cool—Rollerblades. Within about thirty seconds, everything changed as far as my son was concerned. Those roller skates that had been perfectly fine a minute before were now old news. They were embarrassing. No longer would roller skates, the kind his dad grew up on, be good enough.

By the time Brent skated back home he had a full blown case of *But I Really Want It* Disease. Those old skates were thrown in a corner of the garage and the pleading began. "*No one* uses skates anymore Dad" … "I can't be seen out in the neighborhood with those old things on. I'd look stupid" … "Rollerblades are so much faster and cooler, Mom!" … "If I skate around in those old things people will think we're poor." … "But I really really want some rollerblades, Dad." … "Pleeeeeease?"

A Common Malady

There it was. *But I Really Want It* Disease. The craving for something more. Something better. And he wanted it now. Not in two months on his birthday or a year from now. He wanted it now. Just like we want it now.

As I'm writing this, one week ago today iPhone 4S hit the shelves. My daughter immediately traded in her old phone for this newest and bestest phone. I didn't. I was content with my iPhone 4. At least I thought I was. Until I saw her iPhone 4S. Now I find myself trying really hard to be content with my good old iPhone 4. Seriously, have you met Siri? Who doesn't want someone in their life that you can turn to for help anytime you want and they will be there for you. I just have this feeling that she and I could be great friends. So I'm trying to fight off *But I Really Want It* Disease.

The newest and coolest rollerblades? The most advanced iPhone? Any way you look at it, the Gudgels struggle with the disease and my guess is that you do too. Which means there is a high probability that sometime in the near future as you head out on your own, you'll feel the ache for the latest and greatest whatever. And there's a good chance when it hits you'll find yourself thinking and maybe even tweeting or posting…

I've got to get this
I just can't wait any longer
Everyone else has one

It'll be worth the cost
I really want it!

Really? Sounds like Solomon before he got his head back together.

I Messed Up

Ever read the book of Ecclesiastes? It's a book in the Bible that could be appropriately subtitled: *Solomon's Search for Satisfaction.* Solomon was a king whose life started out great. He was good. He was wise. He was wealthy. He had a heart for God. He pretty much had it all together. But when he reached mid life, things took a turn for the worse. *But I Really Want It* Disease took over and messed him up big time.

Little by little, all the great things that Solomon had going for him started to not be enough. *Just one more wife* eventually led to 700 wives and 300 concubines (a concubine was a woman he wasn't married to but he could have sex with any time he wanted to!). And it wasn't just women. Solomon wanted *just a few more* horses and gold and slaves. And the list of things he really really wanted went on and on.

Solomon is considered even by the world as one of the wisest men who ever lived. He's right up there with Confucius and Ghandi. At the end of his life, after his mid life struggle with *But I Really Want It* Disease, he wrote the book of Ecclesiastes, and this is what he concluded. "All man's efforts are for his mouth, yet his appetite is never satisfied" (Ecclesiastes 6:7). No matter how much you have, buy, build, eat, accumulate – it won't satisfy. You'll find yourself still longing for something more.

An Important Lesson Learned

You have the opportunity to learn from Solomon's mistakes without making them yourself. And you can also take a lesson from the Apostle Paul before *But I Really Want It* Disease messes up your life (and maxes out your credit card!). But it's a conscious choice you'll have to make over and over again, because we're all exposed to this disease every day.

Paul wrote a letter to the church in Philippi and said, "I have learned to be content in whatever circumstances I find myself in. I know what it is to be in need, and I know what it is to have plenty. I have learned the secret of being content in any and every situation, whether well fed or hungry, whether living in plenty or in want." (Philippians 4:11b-12)

Can you imagine living with that kind of contentment? In the midst of a world infected with discontentment. When we're confronted by really good advertising everywhere we turn, that makes sure we know about all those really great things that we'd really love to have. When new products are coming out sometimes even faster than we can figure out how to use the old ones! When it's so easy to buy what we want, with what we don't have, with the hope of satisfying something that's yet to be satisfied. When we're constantly struggling with *But I Really Want It!*

Paul experienced that kind of satisfaction and it wasn't based on how much or even how little he had. He said that when he's going through a time when he doesn't have much, he's learned to be okay with that. He's content. And when those times come when he's sailing along with more than he needs, he enjoys it but doesn't take it for granted. He's content.

I once read about a Quaker who watched a young family move into his neighborhood. They had all the toys: two really nice cars, a number of TV's, mobile phones, stereos, jet skis, computers. You name it—they had it. The Quaker, who had learned the art of living with less, strolled over to meet his neighbor and to offer his assistance as they moved in. After spending some time moving around furniture and boxes and all that stuff, in a moment of crazy candor he then added, "Neighbor, if you ever need anything, come see me, and I will tell you how to get along without it."

Not exactly a "how to win friends and influence people" moment, but perhaps exactly what that new neighbor needed to hear. Sounds like what Paul was saying to those who were living in Philippi who had so much stuff and just like us needed to learn the secret of being content.

The Secret Revealed

So what is the secret to fighting *But I Really Want It* Disease? Obviously most people have no idea what the answer to that question is! I guess that's why they call it a secret. But it's something we all desperately need to know.

Millions of people around the world, and especially in the United States, are drowning in debt because they haven't learned to be content in whatever circumstances they find themselves. Unable to curb their desire for whatever is newest or coolest. Constantly spending. Always wanting *just one more thing*. Looking for something that will satisfy them so they'll finally have enough. Yet they end up living full of worry, plagued by unpaid bills, hounded by bill collectors, paying overdraft bank fees... which put them even further in debt!

So what's the secret Paul discovered? What did he learn that we need to learn? Simply this—"I can do everything through Him who gives me strength" (4:13). Paul wrote those words from a prison cell in Rome. Yet in spite of the harsh circumstance he found himself in, he says he's okay with it because the Lord is giving him strength.

And there you have the secret. No matter how much you have or don't have, no matter what circumstance you find yourself in, you have all you need when you have the Lord. And when you stay vitally connected to God, and depend upon His power, you won't need something more than what you already have. Even if what you have is very little.

So the secret is a matter of focus. What is your mind dwelling on? Are you focusing on God and all that He has provided for you, no matter how small it may seem at the moment? Or are you focusing on all the stuff that the world is telling you that you need? Are you trusting God to fulfill the desires of your heart? Or are you looking to get more things to try to satisfy the longings in your soul?

Time to Decide

Some time ago I saw an ad that said, "Yesterday I didn't know it existed; today I can't live without it." That pretty much sums up our problem doesn't it? We're happy with what we have, until something more comes along that's... well—more. And then contentment turns into *But I Really Want It*!

It's at that moment that we need to stop and decide if what we have or don't have is enough. Obviously there are times when new things are good and fun and even needed. But more often than not, we give in to *But I Really Want It* when we don't really need it. And sometimes once we get it, we realize that we didn't even really want it! Which is why anyone who'd like to rid themselves of *But I Really Want It* Disease, would do well to start living out some contentment boosters...

1. Choose to purposefully stay connected to the Lord through on-going time in the Word and conversations with Him. He's the one who will give you the strength to withstand the lure of iPhones yet to be released.

2. Choose to resist the temptation to run out and purchase something you can't afford with money you don't have. To use a phrase from back in the day when I was your age—Just say no!

The bottom line—our desire for more and better is really only our human way of trying to satisfy longings that only God can satisfy. So the next time you find yourself really wanting something more than the things you already have, instead of running to the store, choose to run to the Lord first. Then after you've talked to Him about it, if you decide you want to buy something because you need it, great. But if you realize you want something more and new just to make yourself feel better, forget it. Let God be the one to fill up the longings in your soul.

You need food, but you want steak

You don't have to have a lot to have a lot. (Yes, I meant to say it that way. Read it again if you missed it the first time!) When it comes to wanting more, there are times to say yes, and times to say no. Make sure you are purposefully choosing which situations fit with that.

What do these verses teach you about living with a lot or a little and the inherent dangers or rewards?

Proverbs 30:7-9 — Two things I ask of you, O Lord; do not refuse me before I die: Keep falsehood and lies far from me; give me neither poverty nor riches, but give me only my daily bread. Otherwise, I may have too much and disown you and say, 'Who is the Lord?' Or I may become poor and steal, and so dishonor the name of my God.

How do you feel about living within a budget? Doing so can be a helpful deterrent to unrestrained spending. Thinking ahead, what fixed and flexible expenses do you already anticipate living with?

Fixed Expenses (ie. Tuition, housing, books, food...)	Flexible Expenses (ie. Sports, parties, car, coffee, clothes...)

PART FOUR

TIME
WISE

ten

Purpose

Living for God knows what

LIFE CAN BE so much more than mine was in my freshman and sophomore years of high school when I lived for three things: getting a job, getting a car, and getting a girlfriend – pretty much in that order. My reasoning was simple. I figured if I could get a job and make some money then I could buy a car. And if I had a car then I could get the girl. Surely a girl would prefer a guy who owned a car over a guy who didn't. At least that was my reasoning.

And that triangular three-fold life focus during those years worked. I kid you not. I got a job even though I was only 15 years old. It was a really bad job, but it was still a job. I worked at a butcher shop where my boss cheated the law and me by not even paying minimum wage. But I didn't care. It gave me what I needed: a paycheck and a growing savings account that would soon make it possible for me to purchase my first car.

A Job

A Car

My Purpose

A Girlfriend

That dream became a reality not long after I turned 16 and an older friend of mine sold me a totally cool vintage 1963 Ford Falcon chick magnet. Well, that description isn't completely accurate. It *was* old. But the interior was falling apart. The seats, dash, radio – you name it – were all in sad shape. It needed a ton of work. Especially the paint. It was pea green. Which was pretty ugly. But hey, it gave me wheels and an up on every carless guy hoping to attract the opposite sex. And once I got it fixed up it actually was pretty cool.

So I'd gotten the job and the car. Next on the list was the girl. And believe it or not, my plan actually worked! I don't know if it was the car or me, but what began as a friendship turned into "going steady" and over the next year we had a great time together.

My plan had worked! But I quickly found that the car, the job, and the girlfriend that should have brought me inner satisfaction and fulfillment, didn't. In fact, not long after accomplishing my threefold life quest, I felt utterly bored. I can still remember thinking that something wasn't right about it all.

I was just going through the motions of life each day. The same thing over and over. Wake up—go to school—come home—go to work—come home—do homework—go to bed—wake up… That's pretty much what life was for me, unless it was the weekend when my girlfriend and I went out and cruised the streets of Fresno in my pea green car.

Something's Not Right

Later in life I found out I was going through the same thing Solomon did when he found himself in the midst of his own struggle as he tried to make sense out of his senseless life. This is what he said about it in the book of Ecclesiastes:

> *Ecclesiastes 1:4-8 – One generation goes its way, the next one arrives, but nothing changes—it's business as usual for old planet earth. The sun comes up and the sun goes down, then does it again, and again—the same old round. The wind blows south, the wind blows north. Around and around and around it blows, blowing this way, then that—the whirling, erratic wind. All the rivers flow into the sea, but the sea never fills up. The rivers keep flowing to the*

same old place, and then start all over and do it again. Everything's boring, utterly boring— no one can find any meaning in it. Boring to the eye, boring to the ear.

That was me too. Bored out of my mind. Like King Solomon I felt as if I was on a treadmill to nowhere. Seriously. My life had become the same thing over and over. Tiresome. Repetitious.

Some years ago H.L. Mencken spoke to the predicament my life was in, which so many others also identify with, when he said, "The basic fact about human experience is not that it is a tragedy, but that it is a bore. It is not that it is predominately painful, but that it is lacking any sense."

Boy can I identify with that. That is exactly where I was. Bored and longing for something more, yet unable to find it. And not even sure what *it* was that I was looking for! Until the light went on during my junior year when I had a life-changing aha moment.

There for the Taking

Throughout my high school years I was part of a church, but up until my epiphany I wasn't really all that interested in spiritual things. That's why on most Sundays I either spent the worship hour in the Sanctuary counting the tiles on the ceiling—201, 202, 203…—or hanging out at a nearby A&W with my other bored church friends.

But during my junior year, all the sudden I woke up and realized that life could be so much more than school, my job, my car, and my girl. There was something more that was there for the taking, but not without God. I still wasn't exactly sure what that *more* was, but somehow I knew that I would only find it through my relationship with God.

In looking back on those early high school years, I feel like my life was set on autopilot up until the day I finally decided that God had a bigger purpose for my life. I was just getting up and living each day after day after boring day without really thinking about what in the world I was doing or living for. All I knew was that the job, car, and girl wasn't enough.

It Could Happen to You

But all that changed once I discovered God had a purpose for my life—just like He has for yours. He wants to do more through our lives than we could ever hope or dream. He has plans for each one of us. Coming to see those plans and experience fulfillment in life begins the day we seriously embrace an ongoing relationship with God and determine to know and live out His purposes.

Talk about an infusion of excitement. That is exactly what you can expect once you genuinely turn to God and say, "Lord, from here on out I want every single moment of my life to count. I want to live out the plan you have for my life. Help me live each day doing what You want me to do."

I can guarantee you this, if you pray that kind of prayer and really mean it, God will not only hear you but He'll take you up on your offer. And you'll begin to discover the absolute thrill of living with purpose. So much so that you won't have time for boredom. Your life will become the exciting adventure of following God's leading day after day after day.

The Big Exchange

You want to make the most of your time? You can by making your purpose in life *God's* purpose for your life. It's found in verses like:

> *1 Corinthians 10:31 – So whether you eat or drink or whatever you do, do it all for the glory of God.*

> *Matthew 22:36-39 – "Teacher, which is the greatest commandment in the Law?" Jesus replied: "'Love the Lord your God with all your heart and with all your soul and with all your mind.' This is the first and greatest commandment. And the second is like it: 'Love your neighbor as yourself.'"*

> *Matthew 6:33 – But seek first his kingdom and his righteousness, and all these things will be given to you as well.*

Take a close look at these verses and you'll see God's purpose for our lives. A much greater purpose than the one I lived with before my junior year in high school.

Simply stated, His purpose is three dimensional: It's Upward – a right relationship with God; Outward—a right relationship with others; and Inward—a right relationship with yourself. The remainder of this book will flesh out what each of these areas mean.

But before we get to all that, you need to decide if you're on board with this threefold purpose, which may stand in stark contrast to the one you've been living for. Is God's purpose just a nice idea that's nice for someone else, or is it the kind of purpose that you'd like to have drive your life from here on out?

Solomon finally got on board with God's threefold purpose and in the end it changed everything in him for good. A close examination of the entire book of Ecclesiastes tells his "full of regrets" story, in words that basically say: "Guys, don't do what I did. Save yourself a lot of time, money, pain, and heartache by making a commitment right now to live for God's purpose and not your own. And you'll see that in loving God, and loving others, and seeing your worth through His eyes and not the worldly lens of achievement and accomplishment, you'll experience meaning and satisfaction as you make the most of the time you have to live."

Ready to take that advice to heart? I hope so. I'm sure glad I did. Life hasn't been the same since. It's a whole lot better. I don't count tiles anymore, but I do still drink A & W Root Beer. Just not while ditching church.

Living for God knows what

Take a few minutes to consider and jot down what these verses teach about purpose.

> *Proverbs 16:4 – The* LORD *has made everything for His purpose.*
>
> *Proverbs 19:21 – Many are the plans in a man's heart, but it is the* LORD'S *purpose that prevails.*
>
> *Acts 13:36 – For when David had served God's purpose in his own generation, he fell asleep; he was buried with his fathers and his body decayed.*

What changes, if any, would you have to make to begin living out God's threefold purpose for your life?

- With an upward focus on loving God

- With an outward focus on loving others

- With an inward focus on properly loving yourself

If you have time, take a look at Ecclesiastes 12. How can what Solomon learned keep you from making the same mistakes he did?

eleven

Priorities
Doing first things first

LEXI THOMPSON DIDN'T GO to her high school prom. She didn't have a date. She didn't get to go shopping with her BFFs for the perfect prom dress. She didn't dance the night away with her friends who would all soon be graduating and going away to different colleges.

But you don't need to be sad for Lexi. She isn't. For the rest of her life when new friends ask her what she did for her senior prom, she'll simply say "I didn't go." And she'll be okay with that. Way okay.

You see, instead of doing all the normal high school things, Lexi accomplished something that no one else her age has ever done. She won a Ladies Professional Golf Association (LPGA) Tournament at the "you've got to be kidding me" age of sixteen. And along with that win came a $195,000 check.

Priority Driven
Lexi winning an LPGA Golf Tournament wasn't an accident. No one wins a professional golf tournament by accident. In Lexi's case, she had dreamed about the possibility for as long as she had played

golf, which according to her had been her whole life.

By the time Lexi reached 16, she and golf had been inseparable for more than ten years. The two of them were together all the time: on the lesson tee, at the practice range, at various golf courses. Lexi's faithful and tireless devotion to golf was relentless. She loved it more than school. More than a pretty dress and a prom date.

It became clear at an early age that golf was going to be a priority in her life. In fact, her main priority. That's why her parents decided to pull her out of middle school and enroll her in the Thompson Homeschool. That way Lexi would have more time to pursue her passion. From that day on, her days were devoted to golf until the sun went down, and then at night she'd work on her studies to complete her high school education.

You Have Priorities Too

Lexi isn't the only one living with a set of priorities. You are. I am. We all are. Intentionally... or unintentionally. What those priorities are may not show up on any given day, but a cumulative look at how you spend your time will reveal what they are. Which could be any number of things.

- *Social networking* – time spent on Facebook, texting, using twitter, talking on the phone, or even sometimes actually hanging out with friends

- *Entertainment* – playing video games, watching TV, going to the movies, listening to music, surfing the web

- *Hobbies, sports, the arts* – this is an endless list that could include soccer, baseball, softball, piano, dance, choir, band, painting, cooking, theater...

- *School* – for better or worse, the time required before, during, and after classes

- *Jobs* – whether this be part-time, full-time, or contracted time, you gotta put in the time to get the cash

- *Family* – they'd like to see you, talk to you, and have you do a few chores every now and then

You get the idea. Something or someone right now is a priority in your life. Who or what that is can be seen in what you choose to do or not do with your time. When you look at the schedule of your life, are the things that you spend the most time doing really the things that you want to have as a priority in your life?

Living With Planned Neglect

Several years ago I heard a story about a virtuoso pianist that was asked for her secret to success. She wryly said, "Planned neglect." When asked to explain she replied, "Since I was a child I loved playing and practicing piano. It's been at the center of my life. Along the way there were many other things I could have devoted my time to—sports, boys, even other musical instruments—but I made an intentional *planned neglect* decision. *I planned to neglect* everything else and focus on the one thing that mattered most to me—the piano. I have become the pianist I am today because I intentionally *planned to neglect* other things for this one thing."

Lexi also understood the concept of planned neglect though she probably never thought of it in those words. She made choices that directed her to intentionally neglect some things that could have occupied her time—like a regular school experience complete with proms and football games—so she could focus on her priority, which was golf.

You'd never know it now but I used to play the piano. I actually took piano lessons for five years, from a really good teacher that my parents paid a lot of money for. But now I've pretty much forgotten everything I was taught, due in large part to the absence of planned neglect in my life. I didn't really like playing the piano, so I endured the lessons and put in the bare minimum practicing just so I could tell my parents I had done it. But I wasn't about to give up other parts of my life so I could actually learn to play well. So I spent most of my time doing other things and neglected practicing the piano. Which is why chopsticks is pretty much the extent of my repertoire today.

Your First Priority

Jesus himself spoke to this matter of intentionally choosing how we'll spend our time based on what's most important, in a conversation with two friends, Mary and Martha. In that conversation He plainly affirmed the right priority of one, while correcting the wrong priority of the other.

Mary got it right. She put the Lord and growing in her relationship with Him first. She chose to neglect chores so she could sit at the feet of Jesus when she had the chance. Her To-Do list could wait because her priority was to be with Jesus.

Martha on the other hand was too busy with life in the kitchen. There were things that needed to be done! After all we've got to eat. And she *was* being very helpful. But she was letting life get in the way of what should have been a priority.

It's not that the kitchen wasn't important. It's just that at that particular moment in time, she was missing out on what mattered most—spending time with Jesus. She needed to reorder her priorities. She needed to plan to neglect some things in order to focus on more important things.

Do you know what you want your main priorities to be? And does your schedule reflect those priorities? Or is your day-to-day life actually more focused on other things? Do you need to begin planning to neglect less significant things so you can focus on those main priorities?

If you ask me, making God the first priority in life makes complete sense. But after God, what or who comes next depends on your God-given design and season of life. Our daughter Katie is working on getting her teaching credential. She has one more semester to go, so for the next three months she's choosing to make getting that credential one of her top priorities. And she's choosing to neglect a lot of other things that she normally would love to spend time doing. But instead she's spending her time taking a full load of classes, preparing for state tests, and student teaching five days a week in a Kindergarten class. Fortunately she's single and this all fits her season in life and her calling.

The Sandwich to Success

As you think about what priorities you want to focus on, I'd suggest you give some thought to what I've called the *Sandwich of Success*. Your future success, in whatever you do, will be vitally connected to three key factors: *Time, God, and Talent*.

You want to be a great pianist? A great golfer? A great... something? You must give priority **time** to that endeavor. You must choose to neglect other things so you can focus on that one thing that you want to achieve. Even professional basketball players who've made it to the big leagues will tell you that they still practice shooting hundreds of free throws every week.

I started playing golf when I was in college, so I got a little later start than Lexi. But I enjoy the game and I'm not too bad at it. I'm not great, but not bad. And for a number of years I dreamed of someday making it as a professional golfer. The operative word there is *dreamed*. My life was busy and if I was lucky I'd only get to play golf once every couple weeks.

One day, in a moment of insanity (or hopefully just stupidity), I asked a friend of mine what it would take for me to become a professional golfer like he was. Once he stopped laughing he said, "Well Dave, if you want to get good enough to be a professional golfer you'll need to get up in the early morning and practice from sun-up to sun-down—and keep doing that everyday for the next 100 years." Which was his way of kindly saying "Nice idea but... it ain't gonna happen!"

That's because time in and of itself isn't enough to make a person successful. You also have to be born with God-given **talent**. It's in your genes. It's a gift. If you've ever watched little 5 or 6 year olds playing soccer, you've seen that some of them just get it... and some of them don't. Some things just come naturally to some people. And for other people, not so much.

You and your mom may think you could be the next American Idol, but the truth is if God didn't give you the pipes or the pitch it takes to make it—forget it. You probably wouldn't even make it to Hollywood. The sooner you accept that and embrace your unique design (more about this in chapter 13) the better off you'll be and the less frustration you'll experience.

But if you have the talent it takes to excel in something you absolutely love, and you're committed to putting priority time into it, will that automatically translate into success? Not necessarily, because sandwiched into the center of success is **God**. The one who ultimately is behind the direction our lives take.

I know three different singers who tried out for American Idol. They are all incredible singers. But not one of them even made it past the initial audition. During the first few weeks of each season we see many of the *unusual* people who auditioned and didn't make it. But what they don't show us are the literally thousands of really talented singers that don't make it. Many who have the talent and have put in the time to make singing a career. But for some reason this wasn't their turn to shine.

King David (from the Old Testament) recognized that God is at the center of our success. He spent many years preparing to build the first great temple in Israel. He had the wealth and power and ability and time. But ultimately God left the privilege of building the temple to his son, Solomon.

From David's experience we learn "Wealth and honor come from You [God] alone, for You rule over everything. Power and might are in Your hand, and at Your discretion people are made great and given strength" (1 Chronicles 29:12 NLT). David summed it all up by saying that wealth, honor, power, might, greatness, success…all come from God. While time and talent are key ingredients in success, they are not the most important ingredient. That's God.

Your Planned Priorities

I want to encourage you to think about the things that you want to have as priorities in your life. And remember, some of those priorities will last throughout your life, while others will change depending on the season of life you're in. Then take a look at the things you're putting the most time into. Does your schedule accurately reflect your priorities? If not, it's time to add some planned neglect into your life, and to schedule more time for the things that are truly important to you.

Priorities left to chance and a "whatever I feel like doing today" attitude are sure formulas for failure. Simply floating through life on auto-pilot won't get you very far. And you'll miss out on some great successes that God has planned for you and that He has given you the talent for if you'll only put in the time to make it happen.

Doing first things first

Up to this point in your life, what priorities have driven what you have or haven't done?

Knowing what you do about your talents and desires, what do you think your top five priorities should be?

1. _____

2. _____

3. _____

4. _____

5. _____

Take a look at the Mary and Martha story below in Luke 10:38-42. Which of these two women do you most identity with? What will it take for you to make the Lord first priority in your life?

Luke 10:38-42 – As Jesus and his disciples were on their way, he came to a village where a woman named Martha opened her home to him. She had a sister called Mary, who sat at the Lord's feet listening to what he said. But Martha was distracted by all the preparations that had to be made. She came to him and asked, "Lord, don't you care that my sister has left me to do the work by myself? Tell her to help me!" "Martha, Martha," the Lord answered, "you are worried and upset about many things, but only one thing is needed. Mary has chosen what is better, and it will not be taken away from her."

twelve

Plans

Turn your dreams into reality

I CAN STILL REMEMBER the day I finished my last required PE class in high school. It was a great day! It was awesome to realize that I never had to exercise again unless I wanted to. And for a lot of years, I didn't want to. Except for an occasional round of golf or a couple months out of the year when I played in a softball league… on a team that had no practice required.

But then things changed. A doctor told me to either exercise or die young. So ever since that day I've done some kind of physical activity every day. Yes, every day. On purpose. It hasn't been easy.

I used to hate exercising. I'm pretty sure that started in Middle School when Coach Watson caught me messing around in PE and made me run laps. I can still hear him yelling, "And you keep running until I tell you to stop!" That was not a fun day. I decided around the 5th lap that I was never going to run again unless I was being chased and my life depended on it!

I pretty much kept my no exercise vow until I was in graduate school. Then everything changed after my blood tested in the out-of-whack zone and my doctor told me I needed to turn up the importance of exercise in my life and start exercising everyday. His injunction put me right in the middle of what we've been talking about: Purpose, Priorities, and what we now turn to—Plans.

Up to the day my blood confirmed my need for exercise, I thought I was fine with my *no need to exercise* lifestyle. And the thought of going from practically nothing to exercising every day seemed ridiculous. Not only because I just didn't like to exercise, but also because I didn't know how he expected me to work it into an already busy schedule. So that's what I told my doctor.

He smiled and gave it to me straight. "If you want to live long enough to raise a family and to help people through your life and ministry, you *must* (he definitely emphasized the *must*!), you *must* find a way to change your priorities and plans. You have to find time, everyday, for some kind of exercise. Otherwise from here on out I will need to put you on drugs, and your life will no doubt be cut short, all because you just didn't want to exercise. Do you hear me? Live or die, it's your choice."

Wake Up To A New Plan

It's been awhile since my doctor and I had that conversation. I may not remember his exact words, but I definitely remember his point. And I remember I went home that day and did some serious thinking about my physical health in light of my...

- *Purpose* – Doesn't the Bible say to glorify God with my body? Wouldn't that include staying healthy by exercising and eating right?

- *Priorities* – Right now exercise isn't even on my priority list. Shouldn't it be? Perhaps somewhere near the top?

- *Plans* – Is there a way I can fit exercise into the things I do everyday—like eating, sleeping, and watching TV? Isn't it more important than TV?

You may not need to worry about exercise—yet—but if you think through other areas where you need help in your life right now, in light of your purpose, priorities, and plans, something's probably going to need to change. I know that from experience. After my doctor's admonition and some serious personal consideration, I started working out. I went from no exercise to exercising almost every day. And I've been doing that now for years. But it took an intentional exercise plan that I had to fit in to my already busy schedule.

It's not accidental that the Bible addresses the all-important matter of planning, because most of us are *PC*. And by that I mean *Planning Challenged.* We need to seriously pay attention to what King Solomon wrote in Proverbs 21:5, *"The plans of the diligent lead to profit as surely as haste leads to poverty."*

Give those words a little thought before reading on. Here's Solomon, like a concerned doctor, giving it to us straight when he calls attention to two groups of people: the planners and the procrastinators—headed for two different outcomes: profit or poverty. Your financial trajectory could be going up or down all because of the intentional or unintentional approach you take with planning. A diligent person makes plans and lives by them, a *PC* person has no plans or at the most, in a last ditch effort to get a plan together, hastily scratches out something that *will have to do.*

From PC to PC
When I look at the wisdom contained in Proverbs 21:5 I think about old college friends or colleagues I've worked with through the years. Many of them are honorary members of the National Procrastinators Club, who by the way just announced "Last week was National Procrastination Week." They live by the motto, "Anything worth doing is worth putting off." These guys identify with the kamikaze pilot who flew thirty-three missions.

Actually, all kidding aside, procrastinators are the ones who do all nighters—usually the night before a major test or before a term paper is due. When they work with others, their habit of doing things last minute puts everyone around them in crisis mode because the work they could have done in advance wasn't done, and now it all needs to somehow get done in order to meet a looming deadline that's rapidly crashing in on them. Move this into other areas of your life... not a fun way to live. For you or for those around you!

Solomon says there is a healthier and more profitable way to live. Become PC of another kind: *Planning Competent* rather than *Planning Challenged*. Had I not done that at Westmont in the approach I took to my studies, I may not have graduated from college. And if I hadn't figured out a way to plan to fit exercise into my schedule when my doctor told me to, I might not be sitting here today examining this topic with you.

Three Essential Steps
So what does it take for a person to be the right kind of *PC*? For some of you it just comes naturally. You've been planning out your days and your life since you were three! But for others, not so much. If you're one of those others, assuming you've got your head on straight with your purpose and priorities, here's what I suggest you do.

Step One

Start by putting together an ideal weekly master calendar that allocates time for your top priorities. Here's a sample of what I have in mind:

Time /Day	Sun	Mon	Tue	Wed	Thur	Fri	Sat
6am	Sleep IN!	Get up/Get Ready Prayer and Devotions					Sleep IN!
7am							
8am							
9am							
10a	Church then hang Out	School	School	School	School	School	Home work
11a							
12p							
1P							
2P							
3P	Whatever I want	Exercise	Work	Exercise	Work	Exercise	Work
4P							
5P		Flex time		Flex time		Flex time	
6P		Dinner	Dinner	Dinner	Dinner	Dinner	
7P		Home work	Home work	Work	Home work	Go out with friends	
8P							
9P							
10P							

Keep in mind this calendar is your ideal plan. How you think you could best use your time so you can get in all the things you need to do and want to do.

I'd suggest you begin with your most important priority commitments like God, school, work, homework, family/friends, exercise, sleep, fun… A successful plan must find a way for your priorities to fit into your weekly plan. Said differently, if you can't get your priorities into your weekly plan on paper, you have no chance of living out your priorities in the midst of life's daily pressures and demands.

Step Two

Once you get your priorities into your ideal weekly plan, consider your allocated time slots in light of the commitments and assignments that are before you in the next month or semester. Learning to do this will take a ton of pressure off and will enable you to get the things done that need to get done.

For example, let's apply this step to school. I'd suggest you spread out your assignments over a month or semester of time. Doing this will help you get everything done without going crazy at the last minute and it will give you time to do other things that are also important in your life. And perhaps most important of all, you'll know whether to say "no" or "yes" to other really good things that will undoubtedly come your way and want some of your time.

Here's a simple look at what I have in mind, based on the sample weekly plan I suggested above:

Sun	Mon	Tue	Wed	Thur	Fri	Sat
March Planning Calendar				1 **Read:** Psyc – 40 pg Hist – 30 pg **Write:** Engl – essay	2	3 **Read:** Psyc – 40 pg Hist – 30 pg **Write:** Engl – essay
4	5 **Read:** Psyc – 40pg Hist – 30 pg **Write:** Engl – essay	6 **Projects:** Math – #1-3 Art – project **Write:** Engl – essay	7	8 **Prep:** Psyc – paper Hist – quiz prep **Read:** Engl – fiction	9	10 **Prep:** Psyc – paper Art – read **Read:** Engl – fiction

11	12	13	14	15	16	17
	Read: Psyc – 40 pg Hist – 30 pg **Write:** Engl – essay	**Projects:** Math – #1-3 **Read:** Hist – 30 pg **Write:** Engl – essay		**Read:** Psyc – 40 pages Math – #4-8 **Write:** Engl – essay		**Read:** Hist – 30 pg **Prep:** Psyc – project **Write:** Engl – fiction
18	19 **Prep:** Psyc — midterm Hist – midterm **Write:** Engl – paper	20 **Prep:** Math – midterm Hist – midterm **Write:** Engl – paper	21	22 **Prep:** Math – midterm Hist – midterm **Write:** Engl – paper	23	24 **Project:** Art **Write:** Engl – paper
25	26 **Read:** Psyc – 80 pg **Prep:** Engl – mid-term	27 **Read:** Psyc – 80 pg **Prep:** Engl – mid-term Math – #9-12	28	29 **Read:** Engl – Fiction Hist – 30 pg **Prep:** Art – drawing	30	31 **Prep:** Psyc – term paper Math – #13-18

No question, school can be a huge challenge. But spreading that challenge out over a period of time will make your assignments and responsibilities doable. It beats trying to cram at the last minute. For me, learning to plan in this way made all the difference in my academic performance in college, and to this day has enabled me to stay on top of the myriad of responsibilities in my career and life.

Step Three

A final factor to consider when it comes to plans is execution. You can have the best plans in the world and still fail if you don't actually follow through with your plan. You must have the ability and discipline to put your plan into action. Having hours here and there scheduled to write a paper isn't going to do any good if you don't actually use those hours to write a paper.

I once asked a prominent internationally known pastor for his key to success in his preaching. He could have rambled on about a number of factors: prayer, education, God's providence, walking in the Spirit, spiritual gifts…. But he chose instead to focus on the one area that he has to work at again and again. The *butt factor*. Yes, the butt factor. He said:

> *The key to my success is keeping my butt in the chair until I have thoroughly and adequately prepared myself to teach God's Word.*

In other words, the bottom line for making things happen is to plan your work and then work your plan. It's not going to happen any other way. Plans only jump off the paper and turn into reality when you actually do the work.

I've seen this hold true over and over in my life. When I've wanted to make something happen, I've needed to make a plan and then follow through on that plan. It's not always easy. In fact, for those of us who are naturally *Planning Challenged* it's hard! But it works. It worked for me in college. I got that diploma from Westmont. It worked for me with my health. I've yet to have a reoccurrence of the problem that plagued me when my doctor told me I had to begin daily exercise for the rest of my life. What a difference a plan can make to ensure we're accomplishing the things that are the most important to us.

Turn your dreams into reality

So now it's up to you to make some plans in light of your purpose and priorities. Using the following two charts, map out an ideal plan for implementing your most important priorities.

Time /Day	Sun	Mon	Tue	Wed	Thur	Fri	Sat
6am							
7am							
8am							
9am							
10am							
11am							
12pm							
1PM							
2PM							
3PM							
4PM							
5PM							
6PM							
7PM							
8PM							
9PM							
10PM							

Sun	Mon	Tue	Wed	Thur	Fri	Sat

PART FIVE

CAREER MOVES

thirteen

Design
You're one in a gazillion

AFTER GOD MADE you, He threw away the mold. Not because he thought, "Oh no. That one didn't turn out so good." In fact, if God said anything after making you, it would have been more like, "Wow, now that's another good one."

Incredible thought isn't it? You are one-of-a-kind. Intentionally designed and made with unique looks, personality, abilities, and purpose. Never to be duplicated or mass-produced. God made you specifically and uniquely to be you.

You are one of a kind

I love the thought of that now—God creating me uniquely as I am, on purpose. But for the longest time, especially while in High School, I would have given anything to be someone else. Someone like 'Hoover High star athlete Rodney, who went on to play professional football; or everybody's best friend Jennifer, who lit up a room simply by walking into it; or off the charts popular John, whose magnetic personality and great looks attracted hoards of friends. Those three never ate lunch alone.

And brains? For the longest time I wondered if I had one. Though as I look back, I must have had a lot more going for me in that area than I realized because I made some really smart decisions along the way. Like marrying someone who's a lot smarter than me!

Yes, I can think of a hundred reasons why the high school me wasn't that excited about the person God had created me to be. I would have loved to have come out of a different mold. Someone more athletic, outgoing, popular, and smart. Someone not so much like... me.

Can you relate to that feeling? Or are you more like Lady Gaga, capitalizing on your unique differences. I really do believe the best thing you can do is to be you. The unique one-of-a-kind person God created you to be.

You'd think being you would come naturally. But for pretty much everyone it's a struggle to figure out who we are. It's no wonder the Bible confronts this issue straight on when it says "Do not let the world squeeze you into its mold" (Romans 12:2, JB Phillips translation). Call it peer pressure, the herd mentality, feelings of insecurity, a lack of self-worth, the Barbie Syndrome, or simply the desire to be like someone else you admire. Everyone struggles with it.

Your divine design

Your uniqueness is the focus of Proverbs 22:6 where God gives this counsel to parents: "Train a child in the way he should go, and when he is old he will not turn from it." The words "in the way *he* should go" speak of a child's uniqueness. The person God created that child uniquely to be.

This verse is not telling parents to train their children to fit into whatever mold they, as parents, want for him or her. It's telling them to train their children to recognize and become all that God created them uniquely to be. Discover it, affirm it, encourage it, build on it. Parents do their best parenting when they surrender their will for God's perfect will and design.

Sandy's parents didn't understand this concept. They made that clear when they said "absolutely not" to her dream of becoming a hair stylist and one day owning a beauty salon. Even without any training, Sandy's high school girlfriends flocked to her for help with their hair and make-up because she was so good at it. But Sandy's parents thought her idea of graduating from high school, followed by attending Beauty School was just plain ridiculous. *Their* daughter would go to a four-year college, just like they had, no matter what. And if she didn't go along with their plan, she'd have to move out and try to get by on her own.

And that's exactly what Sandy did. She moved out of her parent's house and moved in with a guy who eventually introduced her to drugs and alcohol. From there she basically dropped off the radar. God only knows what the future holds for Sandy, but so far she's a long way from realizing her God-given potential. She's not anywhere close to recognizing and becoming all that God uniquely created her to be.

This chapter is as much for your parents as it is for you. Someone once said "God loves you and everyone else has a wonderful plan for your life." Your parents, your friends, a boyfriend or girlfriend, the world, your teachers. They all have opinions about what you should do with your life. About who you should be.

So your dad's a rocket scientist? Great! But that doesn't mean you should be. Not good at sports like your friends? No problem. Millions of people aren't all that athletic. Would you rather hang out in the garage tinkering with electronics? Go for it! Apple founder Steve Jobs did—and I for one am grateful. It's a lot easier writing this book on a computer than it would have been with a pencil and a yellow notepad.

Embrace your design

You need to be the person God made you to be and the sooner *you and your parents* get that, I mean really get it, the better off everyone will be. I started looking for my unique design while I was in high school. It seemed pretty clear at the time. The one class I really excelled at, and really enjoyed, was Drafting. As for the others— History, English, Algebra, Science, Social Studies, Spanish—well let's just say I endured them and barely survived them.

But I loved everything about Drafting. Sitting down at a desk and drawing mechanical objects, cars, airplanes, and other three-dimensional things pretty much made my school day. I loved it. My only complaint was that the class was too short. That's why I loaded up my elective schedule with as many drawing classes as possible: Drafting 1 then 2 then 3 followed by Architecture 1 then 2 ... I took them all.

My love for Drafting continued into college. At the time I was sure a career in Architectural Design was in my future. But then out of nowhere, and I mean nowhere, I began to sense the Lord wanted me to pursue a career in vocational ministry. Talk about getting hit by a crazy thought out of left field. No one in my family, and that included me, had any idea that God may have designed me to do anything but design homes for rich people (at least that's what I was hoping). That's why my dad kinda freaked out the night I asked my parents to sit down for a little family chat.

I figured it would be best to start the conversation off with God involved. So after a quick silent "Oh God help me!" I jumped in with "You know how you've prayed all these years that I would become all that God wanted me to be?"

"Yes..."

"Well... all your prayers have really paid off. I think I'm finally getting my act together and I'm starting to feel God's leading on my life."

"That's great Dave."

"Well... I really think the Lord wants me to change my focus in college from Architecture to Sociology so I can prepare for a career in vocational ministry."

I'll never forget what took place next. My father, who up to that point had been sitting, shot up and walked over to a color architectural rendering I had drawn that my parents had proudly framed and hung on our living room wall. It was the best drawing I'd ever done and it gave my parents at least one accomplishment for which they could be proud of their first-born son.

In the two seconds it took dad to get to the drawing I saw his entire demeanor and countenance go from calm and smiling to rattled and glaring. After he raised his right hand and jabbed his index finger into the glass covering my rendering he tersely said, "David, are you telling me that you are thinking about giving this up? A career in Architecture?"

Big gulp. "Well dad, yes."

"For the ministry? Vocational ministry?"

"Yes."

"David, do you know how much the ministry pays in comparison to a career in architecture?"

"Well I know enough to know it will probably be a lot less. But dad, I'm okay with that because I really feel that's what God wants me to do. I think that's what He created me to do."

Then there was silence for what seemed like forever. To this day I still don't know what dad was thinking during that time. In looking back, I'm guessing the Holy Spirit was working overtime right about then! Once he spoke again I was amazed.

"David, if that's what God wants for your life, and that's what He made you for, then that's what I want too. You have my blessing and support."

Those are the words God wants to hear all parents say to their children.

You have my support.
Be what God designed you to be.

So the choice is yours. Your life will be far from wonderful if you're trying to be someone other than the person God made you to be. But if you seek to discover all that He created you uniquely to be, you'll live a fulfilled and complete life.

You're one in a gazillion

Consider for a moment the mold God used when He made you. What is it about you that makes you unique, one-of-a-kind?

Take some time and reflect on the following verses that speak of God's unique design on a person even before they are born. How do these words encourage you?

> *Jeremiah 1:4-5 – This is what GOD said: "Before I shaped you in the womb, I knew all about you. Before you saw the light of day, I had holy plans for you: A prophet to the nations—that's what I had in mind for you."*

Is there anything in your life, or in your relationship with your parents, that needs to change for you to fully embrace your unique design?

fourteen

Experience
Could be your best teacher

UNLESS YOU'RE ONE of the rare ones like Jeremiah or John the Baptist, you weren't born with a handwritten note from God giving you explicit instructions on what the Lord wants you to do with your life. Yet you have something extremely important in common with these two giants of the faith—the Lord designed you, like them, with a unique God-given calling.

Jeremiah's calling was clear. He was born to be a prophet to the nations (Jeremiah 1:5). Talk about an incredible appointment with huge responsibilities and privileges. And with God behind the appointment, Jeremiah didn't dare take his calling lightly.

John the Baptist was specifically chosen by God out of millions of people as the preparatory act before Jesus appeared on earth in the flesh. Call John what you want—forerunner to the Messiah, the leader of the set-up team, a tough act to follow, great in the eyes of God—one thing is for sure, he knew what God wanted him to do, and he did it.

And then there's also King David. The Apostle Paul spoke this fitting epitaph over David's life:

*For David, after he had served the purpose of God
in his own generation, fell asleep… Acts 13:36 (ESV)*

Wouldn't it be great if the same thing could be said of us when our lives are over? David lived out the plan God had for His life. He did what the Lord uniquely designed him for. For someone to say the same of you or me after we die, we must do what David did. Not the kingly stuff, but we need to fulfill the purpose God has for us while living on planet earth.

Discovering our unique design and calling is often the by-product of what our "life experiences" teach us. That was certainly the case in my life when my career path shifted from architecture to vocational ministry,

Thinking one thing while discovering another

Like I said in the last chapter, during high school and my first two years of college, I thought I was going to be an architect. At the time it was the only thing I was good at and really enjoyed. That's why as a college freshman I jumped at the opportunity to work part time at an architect's office.

Although my starting pay as a go-fer wasn't great, I knew the experience I'd get would be worth it and my resume would look a whole lot better when someone saw that I had already worked at an architect's office. For the most part my work there started out with emptying the trash—which I was really good at—and progressed to various drawing projects. It was a great opportunity to get a taste of what an architect's career would be like.

While working at the architect's office, I continued with my junior college education and out-of-the-blue got involved in a ministry to junior high students. Never in my wildest dreams would I have thought there would be a day when I'd join the volunteer staff of Youth for Christ. In the next chapter I'll tell you how that happened, but suffice it to say here, after the Director of Teen Dimension interviewed me, he placed me on his Yosemite Junior High School TD Team. That meant I would meet with a few other leaders a couple times a week to plan a weekly TD Club and then host this after school event for kids who wanted to have some fun and learn about God at the same time.

My involvement in the junior high division of Campus Life continued throughout the first two years I was in college. It meant I spent a lot of time on the campus hanging out with kids and a lot of time hanging out with Mike Reinhold, who not only directed our club but also oversaw seventeen other clubs that met on other junior high campuses. The more I hung out with Mike, the more my respect for him grew, as did my interest in the ministry and his alma mater, Westmont College.

After my first year of college, which included working at the architect's office and ministering with Teen Dimension, the Senior Pastor of the church I attended asked to talk to me one day. He had heard about the work I was doing with Junior High students through Teen Dimension. He asked me if I would consider coming on staff at First Baptist as an Intern to their Junior High ministry. He said they wouldn't be able to pay me very much, but they'd love for me to help out since they thought I would do a great job.

I can remember thinking, "Did he just say *pay*? Like get paid for hanging out with kids? Now that's something I could do!" After taking about 30 seconds to pray over this unexpected job opportunity, I said Yes!

That began a very busy year for me that included my second year in college, working at the architect's office, ministering with TD at Yosemite Junior High School, and now running the Junior High Ministry at FBC Fresno. I later found out my "Intern" title should have been "Junior High Director" because that's what I was doing, only at a fraction of a Director's pay. But it was worth it, because what God did in my life during that year unexpectedly changed my career path.

If I were to graph what happened to me over those ten months, it would look something like this:

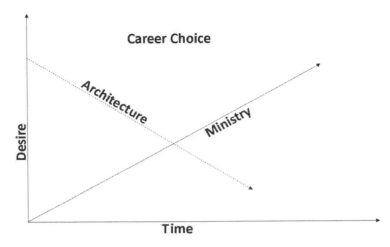

If my life were stock on Wall Street, during that time the value of a career in Architecture began to slowly decline, while the worth of a career in ministry went up and up and up. Like a pot of cold water heating on a stove, I went from vocational ministry not even crossing my mind to realizing that I was meant (created?) to devote my life to the ministry. Something in me changed. I found myself wanting to spend more time with the kids at TD and church. It fulfilled me. In a way that the Architect's office didn't. I gradually came to realize that vocational ministry was what the Lord wanted me to do with my life.

When life takes a turn for the better
One afternoon while sitting at my drafting table in the architect's office where I was working on some very nice house drawings, God spoke to me. Not audibly, but in my spirit in the form of a question. It was as if I could hear Him asking, "Dave, do you want to spend your life designing homes that one day are going to fall down or burn up, or would you rather spend your life working with people and doing something that will last forever?"

I'm convinced God put that question in my mind. When God hit me with that question I was in the final stages of acceptance into the School of Architecture at Cal Poly San Luis Obispo. Attending Cal Poly was something I had been dreaming about for a long time. What I didn't know was that God was steering me onto a completely different career path that perfectly fit with the unique design God had woven into my life.

If you're not familiar with Proverbs 16:9, you should be. This is an extremely important verse to remember while on a career path search. It says, "The mind of man plans his way, but the LORD directs his steps" (NASB). Earlier in this book we talked about "planned neglect." Well this verse is all about "planned flexibility." God is God and we are not, and He alone knows the plans He has for our lives. So any plans we make need to be flexible if we truly want to follow His leading so we can be all He intends for us to be.

When the Lord spoke through Jeremiah He said, "For I know the plans I have for you" (Jeremiah 29:11a). Just as the Lord had plans for the nation of Judah, He also has plans for you. Chances are you may not know those plans yet anymore than I did as a High School or College student. That's why you need to adopt a "planned flexibility" approach to your career search. Plan to be flexible. Go ahead and make your plans and even act on them, but live with an "if it is the Lord's will" (James 4:15) mindset in all you do.

And while you're waiting to find God's clear direction for your life, get out there and get as much experience as you can in areas that you feel drawn to. And keep in mind that the things you're doing right now may not be God's final answer on your career path, but simply a roadside stop to get you to where He ultimately wants you to go.

Get all the experience you can get

Some of the best advice I've received about the importance of experience was this, "Get it. Do a lot of different things. If you think you may be interested in something for a career, seek out a way to try it out. Even if you have to volunteer. You may not know if it's what you're destined for until after you've done it for awhile."

My good friend Art McDonald gave me that advice. At the time I didn't think much of it. Now I know by experience that experience can make all the difference in getting you into the unique work God designed you for.

Ever tried to steer a car that's sitting still? Trust me, it's hard. If you want God to show you your unique design – to steer you to where He wants you to go—then start moving.

Get going in the direction you *think* God has for your life, with a planned flexibility mindset, and see what God does. If you're watching and listening, He'll get you to where He wants you to go. And chances are along the way you're going to discover that which "no eye has seen, no ear has heard, nor mind has conceived ...of all God has prepared for those who love Him" (1 Corinthians 2:9).

Could be your best teacher

In what ways have your past or current experiences helped you discover your unique design?

How would a "planned flexibility" mindset help you right now as you think about what may be in your future?

Proverbs 16:9 – The mind of man plans his way, but the LORD directs his steps (NASB).

Name a few experiences that you'd love to have which could be helpful in showing you the plan God has for your life?

fifteen

Guidance
First look up

GOD IS AND ALWAYS will be the best guidance counselor you can turn to when deciding on your future plans. And I'm not just saying that because I'm a pastor so I'm supposed to say that. I really believe it! You can save yourself a lot of time, money, and frustration if you simply seek out God's wisdom before making decisions about your future career.

Your unique design and experiences are important in discovering what to do with your life, but you also need God's guidance. That makes perfect sense when you consider that God knows your innate design better than anyone because He created you. And He's more than willing to lead you into a career that fits who you are. The Bible gives us this reassurance:

> *Psalm 32:8 – I will instruct you and teach you in the way you should go; I will counsel you and watch over you.*

> *Jeremiah 10:23 – I know, O LORD, that a man's life is not his own; it is not for man to direct his steps.*

> *Proverbs 3:5-6 – Trust in the LORD with all your heart and lean not on your own understanding; in all your ways acknowledge him,*

and he will make your paths straight.

James 1:5-6a – If any of you lacks wisdom, he should ask God, who gives generously to all without finding fault, and it will be given to him. But when he asks, he must believe and not doubt

Ready to help

It seems to me in those verses God is clearly saying He wants to help you, but you have to want His help. He is ready and willing to instruct and teach you, counsel and watch over you, lead and direct you, point out the right path and give you the specific wisdom and insight you need. All you have to do is ask with faith, believing that He will hear and answer your prayers at just the right time.

In my junior year in high school I began asking God to show me what career path I should take. Since asking for His help with other things was something I often did, it was only natural that I'd ask Him to sort out what I was going to do with my life. And if your life is anything like mine was at your age, you can't avoid thinking about what you're going to do with your life because everyone keeps asking you!

It seemed like wherever I went—at home, church, family gatherings, hanging out with friends—someone would inevitably ask, "So Dave, what are you going to do with your life?" Been asked that yet? A hundred times? I'm not surprised. As soon as I hit my junior year, everywhere I went someone wanted to know where I was going to college and what I was going to do with my life. My usual reply was, "I dunno."

Keep on asking

During that time I often found myself repeating the same desperate prayer—"Lord, what do you want me to do with my life?" I really didn't have a clue. So I did what Jesus said to do. I kept on asking and asking and asking (Matthew 7:7) the Lord to show me what I was supposed to do with my life.

Up to that point in time I knew one thing for sure, I didn't want to live my life working in jobs like the ones I had done up to that point: pumping gas at a service station, speeding around town delivering pizzas, working my butt off at a car wash, vacuuming carpets and cleaning toilets at doctors' offices. I was fine doing those jobs while I was in high school, but I was already longing for a better job that would fit the person God made me to be.

While I continued to pray that the Lord would show me what career path to take, well-meaning people continued to barrage me with "So what are you going to do with your life?" questions. If you haven't gotten sick of that question from others yet, prepare yourself. (I guess I should say in their defense that they're only asking because they care about you and they're interested. Try to remember that as you graciously respond to the 100th person who asks you that!)

When the day of my high school graduation finally arrived I was still uncertain about what my future career would be. As I've already said, I did think it might be in architecture, since that was the one thing I had done well and really enjoyed. But I still wasn't absolutely sure what God wanted me to do. What He had created me to do. I never imagined that His plan would begin to be revealed later that night at our Senior Graduation party

Who would have thought?

I almost hesitate to say this, but here goes—after thirteen years of school my senior class celebrated our graduation by having an all night party at a local bowling alley. Yes, bowling. After all the classes, lectures, reading, tests, papers, assemblies, and push-ups were done—we bowled. I don't bowl very often but I actually did pretty good that night. Though I must confess I had an advantage because I was one of the few people there who wasn't drunk.

I spent a good part of the night hanging out with a small group of us who were sober. There weren't very many of us so we stuck together! We talked about a lot of stuff that night since we all felt like we were on the brink of actually getting a real life. One of our own choosing. And that was exciting, but also a little scary. And somewhere in the conversation we eventually came to the "what are you doing with the rest of your life?" question.

Other than Steve, who said he hoped to be a professional golfer, the rest of us didn't have a clue what we were going to do with our lives. And as we commiserated about our cluelessness, an interesting—and in looking back, life changing—thing happened. One of the girls looked right at me and said, "I think you'd be good at Teen Dimension." That was it. That's all she said. Eight words. And then one of the guys added, "Yeah Dave, you should check it out."

I don't remember much more about our Senior Bowling Party but I do remember this—those eight words got stuck in my head. I couldn't get them off my mind. So finally, after two months of thinking about it, I decided to check out Teen Dimension.

Today it would take about two minutes to Google Teen Dimension and find out all about it. But back in those days it took a little more time and effort. Eventually I found out that Teen Dimension was the Junior High campus ministry of Youth for Christ. Which means it was a club that met after school once a week on Junior High campuses. The ultimate purpose was to introduce the kids to Christ, but the day-to-day activities involved simply hanging out with kids and playing a lot of crazy games at our weekly meetings.

Up to that point in time I knew nothing about TD and very little about YFC. That fact made it all the more interesting when I walked into the YFC Fresno headquarters and told their staff I was there because I think God wanted me to check out their ministry and perhaps volunteer to help with TD.

In the years since then, I've learned that God often works that way. He plants an idea in our minds that seemingly came out of nowhere. It's often something that was totally off our radar. We check out the possibilities even though we really don't have a clue what we're getting into. And all of the sudden He's leading us in a direction we never would have dreamed of before.

A word from the Lord?
Eight words at a graduation party. A still small voice in the back of our mind. A word of affirmation or confirmation from a friend. The Lord can and does use any number of things to reveal His plans and will for our lives. And it's always at just the right time. We just need to make sure we're listening.

When I look back now and think about how the Lord decided to answer my "What do you want me to do with my life?" prayer, I'm amazed. Even the person at Youth for Christ who interviewed me when I wandered into their office was astonished. Usually their volunteers were all people who had been one of the kids in their high school ministry and now wanted to come back and be a leader as a college student. But I had never been a part of their ministries before. I had been a Young Life guy. That may have been why they took so much time checking me out.

A clueless high school graduate went to an all night bowling party. God used a seemingly random situation and an out of the blue comment to lead that kid to check out, and eventually work in, Teen Dimension. And his time with TD then led him to be a Youth Ministry Intern at his church. Which led him to go on to seminary for more training. Which ultimately led him into a lifetime of vocational ministry as a pastor. The story of my life.

How does stuff like this happen? God. God planned. God led. God directed. God orchestrated. I'm absolutely convinced this kind of thing happens when we turn to God for guidance and listen for His answer. Especially when we have no clue what to do with major matters like what career to go into.

Sometimes we think, without really thinking, that God's will is something we need to struggle to figure out. Like it's a big secret that He's trying to hide from us. But that is so not true. God wants us to know His will even more than we do! And if we ask Him to reveal it to us, and then listen for His answer, He'll make it clear to us.

God knows what's best
So what does this mean for you now? Simply this. I hope you make a firm decision to seek God's guidance in making a career decision. Don't even try to make this major decision without consulting Him. If God has not made it clear to you what you should do yet, keep on asking and asking and asking for His guidance. It will come. At just the right time. Perhaps when you least expect it. In a random place. In as little as eight words that get stuck in your head. When that happens, follow His lead. Take the next step even if that

step is unsure or doesn't make sense. When you do, God will make your path straight and show you the way He has designed for you to go.

First look up

How would you answer this infamous career question right now: "What do you want to do with your life?"

What would your answer be if that question were tweaked a little to: "What does the Lord want you to do with your life?"

How do these verses assure you that if you turn to God for help, He will give it?

> *Psalm 32:8 – I will instruct you and teach you in the way you should go; I will counsel you and watch over you.*

> *Jeremiah 10:23 – I know, O LORD, that a man's life is not his own; it is not for man to direct his steps.*

> *Proverbs 3:5-6 – Trust in the LORD with all your heart and lean not on your own understanding; in all your ways acknowledge him, and he will make your paths straight.*

> *James 1:5-6a – If any of you lacks wisdom, he should ask God, who gives generously to all without finding fault, and it will be given to him. But when he asks, he must believe and not doubt.*

Can you say you are committed to seeking God's guidance and will for the career you hope to give your life to?

PART SIX

MORAL DILEMMAS

sixteen

Drinking
Is it party time?

WHEN IT COMES TO drinking alcohol, I don't. Not because I can't. I could if I wanted to. But I don't want to. Mainly because I did once and that once was enough to convince me I never wanted to drink again.

At the time I was in my first year of college and some friends and I were hanging out at one of their homes while his parents were out of town. Before that night I had never gotten drunk. In fact, I had rarely even tasted alcohol at all. I had tried a couple beers when I was in high school but it tasted so disgusting to me that I had no desire to drink any more of it. To me it tasted like turtle spit. Not that I actually know what turtle spit tastes like... but if I did, I'm sure it would taste like beer. That's why it was pretty crazy that I got drunk that night.

Somewhere around ten o'clock we decided to raid the refrigerator. That's when we stumbled across a few bottles of beer and some whisky and vodka. With no adults around and the opportunity right in front of me, I decided to try a little whisky. Call it an experiment, curiosity, or just plain stupidity. Like King Solomon "I tried cheering myself with wine, and embracing folly (Eccles 2:3).

Since I was drinking whisky and not wine, I didn't have to drink much before I was full of cheer… for a little while. And while my mind guided me into my drunken stupor, it didn't take long before my stomach was telling me I was in big trouble. I'll spare you the details, but let's just say what happened that night and the next day was awful enough that I said, "I will never do this again." And I haven't.

Alcoholic Consumption

Unfortunately my self-imposed avoidance of alcohol is not the norm. A large percentage of high school and college students drink, not just once or twice to try it out, but again and again and again. For many it's a huge part of their social life. And even though the overwhelming majority of states require a young adult to be at least 21 before they can legally drink alcohol, 3 out of 4 college students drink. For some, drinking is considered one of the most desirable aspects of college life. In fact, 40% of college guys and 30% of girls admit to not only drinking, but also drinking specifically for the purpose of getting drunk. For many, drinking and college go hand-in-hand. It's the norm. In some ways, even expected.

So how does all of this relate to you? If you haven't been forced to make a decision about alcohol yet, there's a good chance that you will in the near future. And that's why it would be a good idea to decide right now where you stand on what could be a very serious issue. And it's just one of a number of issues that you'll be facing in the days ahead as you move out of your parents' home and begin to make life decisions on your own.

In this chapter, and several that will follow, we're going to be looking at some issues where the world's opinion and God's opinion are vastly different. When the world says "Go for it!"— and its opinion may even *seem* to make sense—God is going to offer a different perspective and ask you to follow Him instead of the world.

When the world and God are offering two different paths, and it's time for you to make a choice on which way you'll go, I'd urge you to consider what the right thing to do is in light of two perspectives which stand opposite of each other.

On one side is what *seems right*. It's what the world is telling us to do. And our own minds may even be telling us that it makes sense. This option is talked about in Proverbs 14:12 when Solomon says, "There is a way that *seems right*, but in the end it leads to death."

On the other side is what God tells us *is right*. It's what's best for us based on His understanding and not our own or the world's. The truth taught in Proverbs 11:18b says, "He who *sows righteousness* [does what is right] reaps a sure reward."

What's Right?

What *Seems* Right	What *Is* Right

Two different ways of living that result in two different outcomes, all due to the choices you make. One person does what *seems* right while another does what *is* right.

Do What's Right

So then the big question is, "How do you determine what's *right* when it comes to drinking?" The obvious place to start is, "Are you 21?" If you're not then you will be breaking the law if you choose to drink. And there's no way around the fact that that's wrong. So if your friends or even your own mind are telling you to "Go for it!" remember that you would be doing what *seems* right, but in fact isn't right. And nothing good will come of that.

In a book such as this one, of even greater interest is what God says to us through the Scriptures. At first glance it would seem that the Bible endorses drinking as an acceptable practice. Some may even quote Psalm 104:15 as their favorite Bible verse because it says that God gave wine to "gladden the heart of man." Others would point to Jesus' first miracle as proof that the Lord is not down on wine, otherwise he would have said "no" to his mother's request for more wine when they ran out at a wedding celebration in Cana (John 2:1-10). Some may think that's proof enough for saying it's okay to drink. But before you say "bottoms up," let me suggest you consider three biblical concepts which are essential for sorting out what *seems* right from what *is* right.

Don't get drunk

Without a doubt the Scriptures are crystal clear on the question of drunkenness. It's wrong. It's outside of God's will. Drunkenness is always condemned in the Bible. It's called *debauchery* (NIV, RSV) *dissipation* (NASB), *excess* (KJV), *riotous* (ASV). If you want to experience God's best, His blessing, don't get drunk.

The apostle Paul made this clear in Ephesians 5:18 when he said, "Do not get drunk on wine, which leads to debauchery." In his explicit instructions in the letters he wrote to individuals and churches he went on to condemn drunkenness in this way:

> *Romans 13:13 – Let us behave decently, as in the daytime, not in orgies and drunkenness, not in sexual immorality and debauchery, not in dissension and jealousy.*

> *1 Corinthians 6:9-10 – Do you not know that the wicked will not inherit the kingdom of God? Do not be deceived: Neither the sexually immoral nor idolaters nor adulterers nor male prostitutes nor homosexual offenders nor thieves nor the greedy nor drunkards nor slanderers nor swindlers will inherit the kingdom of God.*

> *Galatians 5:19-21 – The acts of the sinful nature are obvious: sexual immorality, impurity and debauchery; idolatry and witchcraft; hatred, discord, jealousy, fits of rage, selfish ambition, dissensions, factions and envy; drunkenness, orgies, and the like. I warn you, as I did before, that those who live like this will not inherit the kingdom of God.*

Later Peter added these words:

> *1 Peter 4:1-3 – Therefore, since Christ suffered in his body, arm yourselves also with the same attitude, because he who has suffered in his body is done with sin. As a result, he does not live the rest of his earthly life for evil human desires, but rather for the will of God. For you have spent enough time in the past doing what pagans choose to do--living in debauchery, lust, drunkenness, orgies, carousing and detestable idolatry.*

116

It's never the Lord's will under any circumstances for a Christ follower to get drunk. Never. No matter where you live. Not in Ephesus, not in Corinth, not in your city or town, not on your college campus or in your dorm or frat house. Not even, as I learned the hard way, at a friend's home while his parents are out of town.

The fact is, what I did when I got drunk that night was dumb and lucky at the same time. I found out that I didn't like alcohol and that drinking it made me sick! So the decision not to drink became easy for me. But not everyone is like me. Each of us comes into the world with different tastes and tolerances. One of the friends I drank with that night has gone on to struggle with alcohol ever since, and it hasn't been a good thing in his life.

So what do we do with the whole area of drinking? From what I see in Scripture, if you're wanting to follow God's advice instead of the world's, there are two options for you to consider.

Option One: Don't Drink Any Alcohol

There are places in the Bible that point to total alcoholic abstinence. That was the required command God gave in Leviticus 10:8-10:

> *Then the LORD said to Aaron, "You and your sons are not to drink wine or other fermented drink… You must distinguish between the holy and the common, between the unclean and the clean."*

In the Bible this "stay totally away from alcohol" command was directed at three groups of people: Priests, Kings and Princes, and those who took a Nazarite vow of abstinence. Since you probably don't fall into any of those three groups, not much needs to be said here, but the principle behind it is worth considering.

God set this command in place for those in major roles of authority and responsibility. He wanted them to lead with clear minds, pure hearts, and worthy examples. To insure their decisions were made without impairment of any kind by stimulants or substances that would cloud their thinking.

That makes sense to us. And I for one am thankful for similar –
though not as extreme—laws today, especially when I fly. I'm in
complete support of FAA laws that prohibit pilots from flying
while under the influence of alcohol. And though pilots are allowed
to drink at other times, I like airlines that enforce the 24 hour *from
bottle to throttle* standard. It makes complete sense and is a good
thing for all of us who fly.

Aside from the obvious situations where people such as pilots and
doctors and people driving cars and construction workers in very
tall buildings should stay completely away from alcohol, the
principle is also good for us to keep in mind. In the words of the
brilliant physician Dr. Martyn Lloyd Jones, alcohol impedes a
person's "self-control, wisdom, understanding, judgment, balance,
the power to assess everything; in other words everything that
makes a man behave at his very best and highest."

Option Two: Don't Drink Too Much

In the interest of full disclosure, I must admit that the Bible does
endorse drinking alcohol as long as you don't get drunk. Even the
apostle Paul told Timothy, a pastor in training, "Stop drinking only
water, and use a little wine because of your stomach and your
frequent illnesses" (1 Timothy 5:23).

But before you run out and start planning your first trip to a pub
on your 21st birthday, here are three factors to consider that are
implicit in Paul's words, which were written 2,000 years ago in a
very different world:

1. *Wine was safer than water.* Wine was one of the few
    beverages a person could drink in those days without fear
    of sickness or contamination. This is still the case in some
    parts of the world today.

2. *Wine has medicinal value.* This is why Paul told Timothy to
    drink a *little* bit of wine. Apparently Timothy had been
    having some health issues and Paul felt that drinking a
    little wine would help.

3. *Wine was diluted with water.* In biblical times there were two
    kinds of wines: fermented wine (called strong drink) and
    unfermented wine (called new wine). The Bible forbids

strong drink (Lev. 10:9; Prov 20:1; Isa 55:11), while permitting new wine (Gen 27:28). This makes perfect sense because one part of new wine was usually diluted with 3 parts of water. That puts the alcoholic content of new wine around 3-3.5% which comparatively speaking is less than: Beer 4%, Wine cooler 4-6%, Wine 9-11%, champaigne 10%, Brandy 15-20%, and hard liquor 40-50%.

You know what all of that means? It simply supports what Paul told Timothy, a *little* wine mixed with water had its place in that day. It was needed as a beverage and medicinally. Now we can ask if drinking a little alcohol today is needed or desirable in the same or different ways.

My story is simple when it comes to alcohol. I don't drink because I really don't like the taste of alcohol. But what if I did like it? What if you like it? Is it right for us to drink?

The Bible makes it clear that if you want to do what is right, and not just what seems right, you won't get drunk. No question there. And it suggests that there are certain times when we should stay away from alcohol completely so our judgment or abilities won't be clouded or impaired. But aside from those situations, there isn't a black and white answer.

Whether you allow yourself to drink occasionally or you choose to avoid alcohol all together is a decision you need to think through carefully. And I'd urge you to consider the following as you think about the choice you will make. If you choose to drink:

- Will you be able to honor God while doing it?
- Will it be good for you or bad for you?
- Will it harm others around you?

All three of those questions can help you sort out what's the right thing to do for you as a general rule in your life or in specific situations. If you ask me, I'd advise you not to drink at all. But if you choose to let alcohol be a part of your life, I'd urge you to take Paul's advice to heart—make it a *little* drink with just a *little* alcohol in it.

Is it party time?

Up to now, what's been your opinion about drinking? Has it been driven by what *seems right* in your own eyes or by what *is right* in the eyes of God?

How can the teaching of this chapter help you develop or strengthen your convictions about drinking?

Are there other factors than the ones addressed here that can help you know if you should or should not drink?

Who do you know that has a standard on drinking that you respect and would like to follow in your own life?

seventeen

Entertainment
Anything goes?

HANGING OUT IN a hospital Emergency Waiting Room isn't my idea of fun. It's right up there with going to traffic school. I'd rather not, thank you. Which is why I'm glad the day finally came when my wife said, "Dave, it's a bad sign when the emergency room staff know you by name. From now on you're not allowed to play soccer... or softball. And don't even think about taking up basketball or flag football. You're done."

She was right. My aging body didn't bounce back like it used to. And even though my participation in recreational sports was limited to a few occasions here and there, I still somehow kept finding ways to get hurt. A hand fracture here, a pulled Achilles over there, here a wrenched ankle, there an aching back.

Well you get the idea. I was making way to many trips to the emergency room. So my loving wife banned me from the sports that were sending me there. And it worked. I spent a lot of years without making a single trip to the emergency room. Until one day when I was unexpectedly hit by "chest discomfort."

I wish I had known to use those two words—chest discomfort—

on all my previous emergency room visits. I now know it's the fastest way to totally bypass the waiting area where in the past I had spent hours waiting to see a doctor. But this time, as soon as I said those two words I was shoved into a wheelchair and immediately taken to an examination room where I was met by a doctor who started asking me a bezillion questions: "What do you feel? Where do you feel it? How long have you been feeling this way? Have you ever felt this way before? Any previous heart problems? How about gastric related problems?"

After all the questions, a quick exam, and an EKG, the doctor said, "From what we've seen so far, we're not sure what's causing your chest discomfort. It could be heart related or it could be gastric related. It may be nothing more than heartburn, but the only way to be sure is by doing some additional tests."

"Great, "I said, "Let's get it done so I can get out of here. I have a couple of hundred other things I need to do today!"

He then informed me that the tests I needed to have done were usually scheduled for mornings. Which meant that they needed to admit me and keep me overnight. When I told him I'd be happy to come back in the morning, he replied, "That's certainly an option but… I wouldn't recommend it because if your chest discomfort is heart related, and you were to have a heart attack sometime before tomorrow morning, you could die. So I would suggest you stay here overnight so we can monitor your heart."

So much for a short hospital visit. I stayed there that night and went through a full gamut of tests the next day that fortunately revealed my heart was in great shape and that the discomfort must have been gastric related. Boy was I grateful for how things turned out for me physically, and now as I look back I'm also thankful for the spiritual lesson the Lord taught me that night as a very competent hospital staff monitored my heart. I've since come to realize how important it is that we do this 24/7.

YOU Must Protect Your Heart

Did you know that the Lord, the greatest doctor of all time, advises us to constantly monitor our hearts? Proverbs 4:23 zeros in on the importance of this when it says, "Watch over your heart with all diligence, for from it flow the springs of life" (NASB). When Solomon said those words, he wasn't talking about our pulse rate or cholesterol levels. He was saying that we each need to be concerned about the well-being of our heart which includes our mind, soul, and feelings, because the condition of our heart affects our entire life.

Do you ever consciously monitor the health of your heart? Do you evaluate what's going on in your mind where no one else can see or hear you? Do you monitor the things you let your eyes and ears bring into your soul?

King David did. In Psalm 101:3 he said, "I will set before my eyes no vile thing." He purposely chose to not let anything into his heart or soul or mind that could lead him in the wrong direction. And when you think about how different his world was from ours, it makes it even more important for us to guard our hearts.

Two thousand years ago David and Solomon didn't have television or movies or the internet or video games. If they wanted to see or do something inappropriate, they had to go out and look for it. Or I guess they could have it brought to them since they were both kings. And yet even then, they knew how important it was to guard their hearts.

But today we've got it even harder. Though we're not kings, we can find pretty much any kind of entertainment we want without even leaving the privacy of our home or dorm room. And no one but God will know. With just a few clicks on a keyboard we can satisfy any desire we might have for a good laugh, a good feeling, a fantasized desire. With one click of a remote we can expose our hearts and minds and very souls to anything that entertains.

We live in a day and age when we are surrounded by limitless opportunities to be entertained. My digital cable TV alone has literally thousands of channels. And the possibilities on the internet —even through our phones!—are limitless. If you want to see it or experience it or feel it, it's right at your fingertips.

Now I'm not down on television or movies or the internet. That type of technology has opened up some awesome things to all of us. And great good can be done through it. But it has also opened the door for all of us to be influenced by many things that can defile or damage our hearts. And often, disguised as "entertainment," we may not even realize it's happening.

This Is Your Responsibility

I spin. Not in circles, because that makes me sick. I spin on a stationary bike. Twice a week I attend a cycling class at a Fitness Center. Of all the exercise I do, this one is the most intense and it's the one that's best done while wearing a heart monitor. Spinning can easily get your heart rate up way too high. In fact, so high that if you're not careful your heart could be damaged by the intensity of the workout.

Over the seven years that I've been going to these spinning classes I've learned that I have to pay close attention to my heart rate monitor. Which means that sometimes when the instructor yells for us to "CRANK IT UP A NOTCH!" I need to just ignore him. (Though I'll admit that sometimes I reach down to the nob and *pretend* I'm cranking it up!) For my own health and safety I'd rather pay attention to the condition of my heart than blindly follow my spinning instructor in an attempt to stay up with those around me.

The Lord has given us a heart monitor that we'd do well to strap on and pay attention to. It will protect our hearts from harm and give us the life we seek. This fail-proof heart monitor is found in Philippians 4:8 where it says: "And now, dear brothers and sisters, one final thing. Fix your thoughts on what is true, and honorable, and right, and pure, and lovely, and admirable. Think about things that are excellent and worthy of praise."

The Perfect Heart Monitor

Near the end of Paul's letter to his friends in Philippi, he encourages them to protect their minds, which could also be called their hearts. In so doing he gives us a grid that can be used for screening out the bad from the good. I've found turning his advice into a series of eight questions can be helpful when determining what you will let yourself be entertained by:

1. Is this *truthful*? Is this a reflection of the truth taught in God's Word or is it undermining God's Word with humanistic thinking?

2. Is this *honorable*? Can I give God glory by watching this? Will God be honored? Will seeing this please Him?

3. Is this *upright*? Are the values taught in-line with God's values? Will what is said and done be a reflection of what *seems* right in the eyes of man, or what *is* right in the eyes of God?

4. Is this *pure*? Will this arouse sexual thoughts or desires? Will this cause me to lust after that which is immoral?

5. Is this *beneficial*? Will I walk away saying, "That was worth my time and money! It was great. It's going to help me be a better person."

6. Is this *admirable*? Is it worthy of respect? Do the storyline and the values reflected inspire me?

7. Is this *excellent*? Is it of the highest or finest quality?

8. Is this *recommendable*? Will you be able to without reservation recommend this film, TV show, game, or website to others? Or would you be more inclined to hide it with the hope that they never find out what you've been watching?

That's an incredible list of questions, isn't it? Protective? Absolutely! A great way to monitor your heart and guard it from harm. A very practical checklist to help keep your eyes and ears away from things that will defile and damage your life.

Put It To Use
Of course it's one thing to own a heart monitor, it's another thing to actually strap it on and use it. Up to this point in time can you say you've done a good job of guarding your heart from harm? Have you used the 4:8 checklist or one like it when making entertainment decisions? Or have you just gone with whatever you felt like at the time?

If you're on board with the Lord's heart monitor, if you want His standards to be your guide for what you let into your heart and soul and mind, then putting it into practice is up to you. One thing's for sure, the rating system (G, PG, PG-13, R, NC-17) isn't a sure guide when deciding what to see or not see. Whatever the rating, it's a good idea to read reviews before you grab your popcorn and soda and head into the IMAX theater where you can't miss seeing and hearing whatever they put in front of you.

Two years ago a young friend of mine named Mel had an unexpected heart attack. It almost killed him. Actually it did kill him. Seventeen times. Had it not been for the paramedics and a team of doctors who shocked his heart thirty-three times over a twelve hour period of time, he would have died—for good. His heart would stop. They'd bring him back. Thirty-three times.

Mel is alive and well as I write this chapter. But the Mel I know today is a lot different than the Mel I knew before. He's made significant changes in his life for the sake of his heart's well-being. For one thing, Mel's diet has totally changed in an effort to reverse the damage he had done before. He's controlling what he's taking in for the sake of a better future for he, his wife, and their six children.

In a similar way, everything we let in to our hearts and minds will affect who we are. Every television show or movie we watch. Every song we listen to over and over until we know it by heart. Every video game we play. Every website we visit. So one of the best ways to make sure we stay strong and healthy and whole is to guard our hearts. I hope you will consider strapping on a heart monitor and using it 24/7 to help you control the entertainment you're letting influence your life.

Anything goes?

Are you on board with your need to monitor your heart? Do you want to do that? Why or why not?

On the chart below, list the past five movies or TV shows that you've seen? Would you give a "yes" or "no" when you consider what you saw through the 4:8 evaluative grid?

Was it...?	Show:	Show:	Show:	Show:	Show:
truthful?					
honorable?					
upright?					
pure?					
beneficial?					
admirable?					
excellent?					
recommendable?					

What specific steps do you hope to take to guard your heart from entertainment that could harm it?

eighteen

Gambling
Worth the bet?

AS FAR AS I KNOW my mom and dad weren't addicted to gambling, but they gambled every time our family vacationed in Las Vegas or Lake Tahoe. They called it recreational gambling. My dad *played* Blackjack and my mom *played* slot machines.

"We're just going inside Harrah's for a few minutes to have some fun," they'd say as they left me in the car to babysit my two younger brothers and sister. That was not much fun for us kids, especially since we were in Las Vegas where it can be blazing hot in the summer!!

When we got older, but still not old enough to go in and gamble, we'd stand outside the casino staring in through the windows. We couldn't see much, but we were fascinated by the hoards of people we saw jamming money into what looked like vending machines but they weren't getting much back out of them. I can remember thinking that it sure didn't look like they were having much fun. In fact, most of them looked mad.

And the same was true for my parents. Most of the time when they came out of the casino after *playing*, they were in a pretty bad mood.

And as we drove away they would usually end up arguing about anything and everything—who had lost the most money, what we were going to eat for lunch, where we were going to stay that night, and how much money this stupid vacation was costing.

They went in with high hopes of having fun, *playing* a few games, and winning money that would help pay for our vacation. They usually came out frustrated and angry. And us boys often ended up sleeping outside the car by the side of the road instead of in a hotel.

My parents never intentionally taught us kids anything about gambling. Maybe they figured we wouldn't want to gamble simply because we saw the arguments gambling led to, followed by screwed up vacations and us boys sleeping in the dirt next to our car. Or maybe it just didn't even cross their minds that one of us kids could end up with a serious gambling problem. But their example, and the people I saw through the casino windows, convinced me that gambling really wasn't all that much fun.

I'm guessing that you haven't done much gambling at this point in your life. But it may be in your near future. It seems to be the new trend that for Bachelor Parties or when people turn 21 they go to Vegas with a group of their friends. And at that point, choices need to be made about not only drinking but also gambling.

I'll admit right now that you won't find an eleventh commandment in the Bible that says, "Thou shalt not gamble." If there was, this discussion could end right now with a simple, "If you want to do the right thing—don't gamble. Gambling is a sin. One of the big eleven. Don't do it. Any questions?"

But since that isn't the case, we need to spend some time discussing whether gambling is a good idea or not. Perhaps the following three questions will help.

Why Do You Want To Gamble?

Asking a question like *Why do I want to gamble?* can be helpful in revealing your motivation for gambling. Yesterday I was on an airplane with a loud, rowdy bunch of people who were on their way to Vegas. It wasn't my place to ask them why they were going, but I'll bet (pun intended) they would have said they were going to Vegas to have fun. Just like they'd spend a little money to go to a movie, or out to dinner with friends, or to Disneyland. And of course maybe while they're at it they'll win some money too, which would make it even more fun.

Hard to argue against that, right? I'm all for having fun. And I'm willing to spend some money to do it. In fact, I spend quite a bit of money each year following a little white ball around a golf course all in the name of fun.

I like the "permission to have fun" verses found in the Bible like Ecclesiastes 5:19 that says, *It is a good thing to receive wealth from God and the good health to enjoy it. To enjoy your work and accept your lot in life—this is indeed a gift from God (NLT).* God wants us to have fun and enjoy life. He even makes it possible through the wealth and health He gives us.

The fact is there's nothing wrong with having fun. So honestly, I'd have to say that there's nothing wrong with taking $20 into a casino and *playing* until the $20 is gone. If you win some more money, great. If you lose your $20 and then call it quits, that's okay. As long as it was fun.

But it becomes a problem when something else takes over. If you come out angry or frustrated. If your desire to win (greed?) causes you to spend a lot more than you had originally planned.

When greed takes over and the desire for *just a little fun* turns into the desire for more and more money, the abundant life God offers is choked out of our soul and a person is set-up for a lot of trouble. Paul spoke to the issue of greed and its consequences when he said:

> *For the love of money is a root of all kinds of evil, for which some have strayed from the faith in their greediness, and pierced themselves through with many sorrows. (1 Timothy 6:10 NKJV)*

The following words were written by a person who found this awful reality out firsthand as he became obsessed with gambling:

In one way you are trying to buy happiness but so many times all you get is misery. It's the hardest thing in the world to be content with what we win because of the human condition…All humans are basically greedy.

That could happen to anyone. So I'd urge you to ask yourself this: If there was no possibility of winning, would you still gamble? Would you be totally satisfied with spending $20 for a little bit of fun and nothing else? Or is there something inside you that really wants to come out of the casino with a lot more money than you went in with? Why, really, do you want to gamble?

Are The Risks too Risky?
Are you a risk seeker or do you prefer to play it safe? Are you excited by things where you're trying to beat the odds or do you like to stay in control? We've all heard how the odds in any casino are in the favor of the house. If they weren't, casinos would go out of business. They've got to be taking in more money than they pay out or they'd have to close their doors. But the risk I'm talking about goes beyond the odds of losing some money.

Statistics show that one out of twelve people who try a little gambling end up becoming compulsive gamblers. What started out as just a little fun becomes an addiction. A very expensive and often dangerous addiction. Take it from this guy who said:

I am a nineteen-year-old male. I do on-line sports gambling. I started off with small bets. When I lost I didn't think much of it, but now I'm always trying to get money back. My average bet is a few hundred. I feel sick and empty when I lose and feel I must win it back…I just like gambling. I'm trying to stop now…I would warn anybody reading this who is going to start gambling to not think about even starting it. Sure it can give you a buzz, but when you lose you feel empty and worthless.

He's one of the one out of twelve who never should have even set foot inside a casino. Of course, at the time he was probably like you in that he thought he was just going in to have a little fun. No big deal. I'll spend $20 and then I'm outta there.

Most gambling addicts don't realize they have a problem until it's already become a serious addiction that will be as hard to kick as any other compulsive behavior. It starts out just for fun. Then they actually win some money! Which makes them think they can win even more money. But inevitably they start losing more than they're winning. (Remember, the odds are not in your favor) But they can't stop because they have to win back the money they've already lost. And so it goes on and on.

Even without going to Vegas, we've all seen the Strip on television and in movies. The huge casinos and resorts and fountains and bright lights are incredible. Millions of people wander the streets and visit the casinos there every year. The amount of money it takes to build and maintain and run those places is overwhelming. Where do you think that money comes from? When those people sit down at a gaming table or a slot machine, who do you think wins?

A deck of cards has fifty-two cards in it, thirteen cards in each of the four suits. Your chance of drawing the card you want is 1 in 52. Your chance of getting a perfect poker hand is 1 in 2,598,960. Interested in a game where dice are thrown? Each die has six sides so the chances are 1 in 6 that you'll throw the number you want. But the chances are 1 in 216 if you throw three dice.

Fascinated by slot machines? The typical slot machine pays out $5,888 for every $8,000 put in. Slot machines are actually the most addictive form of all gambling. Nearly 40 million Americans play a slot machine each year, and the owners of those machines ended up grossing more last year than McDonald's, Wendy's, Burger King, and Starbucks combined.

Is it worth the risk? Of your money? No. Of your life? Attend a Gamblers Anonymous meeting, where you'll hear story after heartbreaking story from well-meaning people whose lives today are totally messed up because they got hooked on gambling. Their relationships and finances are a wreck and if they're Christians, their walk with God is messed up. Do you really think gambling is worth putting yourself at risk knowing any or all of the above can happen to you?

Will It Be Worth It?

Every financial decision is also a spiritual decision because you are using God's money. God owns it all, including the money He's entrusted to your care. What you do with the money you have will reveal who's controlling your life – God or money. What we do with the resources God gives us will reveal what's most important in our lives. The Bible alerts us to a day that is coming when we must give an account of how we used the resources God gave us.

> *Luke 16:1-2 – Jesus told his disciples: "There was a rich man whose manager was accused of wasting his possessions. So he called him in and asked him, 'What is this I hear about you? Give an account of your management, because you cannot be manager any longer.'* "
>
> *1 Corinthians 4:2 –Now it is required that those who have been given a trust must prove faithful.*

Now's the time, before you insert even a nickel into a slot machine, for you to determine if gambling has any chance of being worth it when it comes to…

- Using God's money wisely?
- Putting yourself at risk?
- Giving yourself something fun to do?
- Potentially hurting others?
- Hurting your relationship with God?

So what are you going to do? Will you or will you not gamble? You really do need to think this through before you do something that you could later regret.

Worth the bet?

Still not sure if you should gamble or not? In addition to the above three questions, consider the following.

Will gambling help me glorify God? (Can I do this and still please God?)

> *1 Corinthians 10:31 — So whether you eat or drink or whatever you do, do it all for the glory of God.*

Will gambling be profitable? (Does the upside outweigh the downside?)

> *1 Corinthians 6:12a — All things are lawful for me, but not all things are profitable...*

Can gambling control me? (Will it take over my life?)

> *1 Corinthians 6:12b — All things are lawful for me, but I will not be mastered by anything.*

PART SEVEN

SEX
MATTERS

nineteen

Hooking Up
Not that big of a deal?

TEN MINUTES AGO I hooked up… NOT in the way most college students think. I simply hooked up my laptop computer to my desktop speakers. No big deal really. We hook up around the Gudgel house all the time. Last week I hooked up our wireless router to our AT&T Cable connection. The other day I hooked up our garden hose to a front yard faucet. Every year I hook up about a million Christmas lights to electrical outlets. And as often as we can, we love to hook up our propane tank so we can enjoy an outdoor BBQ. Hooking up is something we Gudgels seem to do a lot.

Of course hooking up today has an entirely different meaning than the Gudgel behavior I've just described. Nowadays when a younger person talks about "hooking up" they have something else in mind entirely. Here are some current definitions of hooking up:

Making out

Having sex with no strings attached

A "one night stand" with someone you aren't in a relationship with, and may barely know, simply for fun and sexual satisfaction

137

Usually described as a sexual relationship with no strings attached, hooking up can refer to a gamut of behaviors that run from kissing, to sexually touching, to full-on sex—most likely with someone you're not in a serious relationship with. Casual sex. Just for fun.

Whatever physical activity a person associates with hooking up, one thing is sure, today it's a *normal part of the college experience*. At least that's what a growing number of college students are now saying:

> *It's a part of college life at the moment. People hook up and it's no big deal.*

> *They move on and act as if nothing happened.*

> *It's no big deal. It's part of college life. I think that people make it too big of a deal sometimes.*

A normal part of college life that's *not that big of a deal?* Simply a fun and enjoyable way to find immediate pleasure and sexual satisfaction with no residual consequences? Not according to this gal:

> *I'm only 20 years old and I've hooked up with more guys than I can count on fingers and toes. The guys weren't anything, weren't friends, weren't boyfriends. It was purely for physical fulfillment. I wanted to feel good physically and I wanted to be wanted. I wanted to have someone's attention... I knew the consequences. The emotional and spiritual ones. The ones that make you feel separated from God— that make you feel empty, guilty, lonely, angry, sad, selfish. The consequences of defiling your soul.*

> *I wanted pleasure, I wanted wholeness, yet all I got was broken relationships, emotional issues, and a reputation with a capital S. It wasn't worth it, and I'd never recommend it. I hooked up because I thought it could satisfy. It just made me more broken.*

Only one side of the story, you say? You're right. Here's an entirely different perspective on hooking up:

> *Casual consensual sex has no negative effects on your health. You may argue that it has negative effects on your emotions but, as someone who knows a lot of people (male and female) who have*

casual sex regularly and a lot of people who don't, I have to say that (anecdotally) I cannot see any of these negative effects—indeed if anything the reverse is true. The thing is, as a university student, I live in an almost entirely non-religious environment. Sex is not treated as a big deal at all among the people I mix with so the negative effects born again Christians talk about are not manifested. It seems to me that the guilt people feel about premarital sex, and the emotional issues that result from it, are due to the unnatural repression of sexual urges by adherence to religious dogma. The solution, then, is not to give up sex until you get married, but to cast off the shackles of slavery to an invisible, almost certainly nonexistent desert god and embrace human life and enjoyment in all its richness.

So there you have it. Two different people with two different viewpoints. Both with first hand experience in the whole hooking up culture. One says hooking up is a big deal. Another says it's not. So which is it? Should a person seek satisfaction for their sexual needs through a hook up? Is it just another form of entertainment like going out to dinner or a show? Or is it more than that?

The body is for sex

Anyone living in Corinth during the first century also faced what we face in the twenty-first century. When it came to determining whether a hook up was the right or wrong thing to do in that world, one person "said this" while another "said that." While in the first century getting together with someone for sex wasn't called a hook up, that's precisely what it was. A natural way to sexually satisfy a normal physical need—like you would satisfy your hunger by eating food.

People in the first century lived by the hedonistic slogan, *like food is for the body and the body is for food …sex is for the body and the body is for sex*. The Corinthians viewed eating and having sex as natural bodily functions to satisfy as needed. Like the body needs food, the body needs sex. So sex wasn't a big deal. It was just something you did to gratify your sexual cravings like you ate food to satisfy your stomach's growling. So…eat, drink, and be merry! Forget guilt. Ignore what others may think or say. Embrace unrestrained sexual freedom for the sexual satisfaction you need. Even Roman law endorsed prostitution as a legitimate means for getting the sexual satisfaction one sought. The light was green for hook ups in red light districts and beyond.

The similarities to today's world are clear when you hear a guy say, "My sexual needs are just like my need for food. If I get hungry I drop by McDonalds for a quarter pounder with cheese, and if I feel a need for sex I get a date with a girl who is willing. As long as we both want to do it, I don't see anything wrong with that."

Recently I was told by my doctor that I needed to get my antioxidants up by eating more fruit, like blueberries. So I went on a blueberry hunt at *Trader Joe's* and found some really good organic blueberries. But then I turned the corner and found dark chocolate covered blueberries. Now follow my thinking on this: If blueberries are good for me, and dark chocolate is also good for me, wouldn't that make blueberries covered with dark chocolate even better?

As much as I'd like to buy into that line of thinking and eat to my heart's content, that kind of thinking has trouble written all over it. I could end up gaining 10 lbs on my path to better health! One thing (blueberries) doesn't legitimize scarfing down the other thing (dark chocolate covered blueberries) even though I may wish it did. It will only hurt me in the end. In a similar way, thinking that legitimizes satisfying your sexually cravings like you satisfy your hunger cravings is a set up for disaster.

The body is for the Lord

Like a caring doctor, the apostle Paul wisely tells these professing Christ-followers living in Corinth to reject what *everyone else* was doing, for a healthier lifestyle. This is what he said to the Corinthians caught up in the cultural mindset of their day:

> *You say, "Food was made for the stomach, and the stomach for food." (This is true, though someday God will do away with both of them.) But you can't say that our bodies were made for sexual immorality. They were made for the Lord, and the Lord cares about our bodies... Don't you realize that your bodies are actually parts of Christ? Should a man take his body, which is part of Christ, and join it to a prostitute? Never! And don't you realize that if a man*

joins himself to a prostitute, he becomes one body with her? For the Scriptures say, "The two are united into one." But the person who is joined to the Lord is one spirit with him... Don't you realize that your body is the temple of the Holy Spirit, who lives in you and was given to you by God? You do not belong to yourself, for God bought you with a high price. So you must honor God with your body.
1 Corinthians 6:13,15-17,19-20 (NLT)

Paul's straight forward appeal is simply this, "You've adopted the wrong slogan for life. Replace your *sex is for the body and the body is for sex* way of living with *the body is for the Lord and the Lord is for the body.* The real you resides in your body that was designed by God to bring Him glory, which it will do when you value and protect your body like Christ would. Simply stated, this is what that means:

- God is the maker, owner, and occupant of your body. Actually your body isn't your body. It's God's. You're the body's caretaker.

- What you do with your body will honor or dishonor God. God wants you to honor Him with your body. God is not honored when you sexually hook up. He calls it sexual immorality. He calls it sin.

- A hook up is more than a physical act. It unites all of you—your body, soul, and spirit—to another person. You can't just physically hook up and be done with it. The Message Bible translates this thought this way: *There's more to sex than mere skin on skin* (1 Cor 6:16a).

- A hook up is a blatant sinful disregard for the body God resides in. Like Christ would never, never, never hook up and thus defile His body, neither should you as the caretaker of His body.

- Honor God with your body by not hooking up.

- A hook up is a BIG deal.

When I consider the wise counsel Paul painstakingly gives here, I see it in light of a San Francisco apartment I've been privileged to use while writing this book. Talk about an incredible place to stay and write! My view from the twelfth floor of this apartment building includes San Francisco, the bay, and the Bay Bridge. Throughout the day I see city and sea life. It's inspiring. At night through the sliding glass doors my eyes are drawn to the lights that sparkle off the buildings around me which then end up reflecting off the nearby bay in front of me. I could sit here and stare at it for hours.

This cute one-bedroom apartment that a really nice couple allows me to use comes with a reasonable expectation—enjoy the apartment but also take care of it as they would. What that means isn't hard to figure out. Simply stated: Don't trash the apartment. Keep it clean. Protect the valuables they've placed in it. Replace what I use or break… You get the idea. I don't own this place. I'm just a temporary caretaker of another family's bayside home. What I do here, how I treat that which isn't mine, will either honor or dishonor my gracious friends. For me, that's more than enough incentive to treat their home in a way that shows these really nice people the respect and honor they deserve.

And so it is with the body God's given you the privilege of living in and caring for. Will you honor the Lord with your body by only using it the way Jesus would? Will you see your body as more than just flesh & blood, but a very special house in which God dwells? Will you say no to hooking up?

Yesterday the couple who leases this apartment gave me a great report. They told me I've been the best guest that's ever used their bayside home. They said, "Dave, you leave our home cleaner than anyone ever has." That may not seem like a big deal to you, but to them it is. And if it's a big deal to them, then it's a big deal to me.

Keeping your body clean by not hooking up is an even bigger deal to God. So the choice comes down to you. Are you going to follow the prevailing view of society that hooking up is just natural and fun and not a big deal? Or are you going to trust that God knows better?

Not that big of a deal?

Reflect on the hook up culture you live in and how you will respond in light of the following biblical thoughts set forth in 1 Corinthians 6:13-20.

But you can't say that our bodies were made for sexual immorality.

Don't you realize that your bodies are actually parts of Christ? Should a man take his body, which is part of Christ, and join it to a prostitute? (Like a hook up, sex with a prostitute was a means to sexual satisfaction)

Don't you realize that if a man joins himself to a prostitute, he becomes one body with her?

twenty

Abstinence
Old-fashioned and out-of-date?

I'M GUESSING the last time abstinence showed up on a "hot topics for conversation" list, people were writing books like this one on typewriters. Today both things could be considered nostalgic. Retro. Ancient history. Something sweet from a simpler time in the past. But definitely out of date.

When I was in college a pastor at my church gave me some advice when I was thinking about taking typing as one of my General Ed classes during my first two years of college. He told me I should *not* take that class! He *said* it was a bad idea. He said that if I didn't know how to type, any church I worked at in the future would have to give me a secretary... since I didn't know how to type.

His advice at the time sounded great—so I took it. I never took a class to learn to type. Unfortunately, I had no idea that in the very near future, even though typewriters would end up on dusty shelves in antique shops all over the world, personal computers with *typewriter keyboards* would become the center of all our word processing... and emails... and ordering things online... and social networking... In the 21st century, computers—and typing on them —have become indispensible.

I do have an Administrative Assistant now (we don't call them secretaries anymore). I also have an old typewriter in a storage shed somewhere, and a lap top computer and an iPad and an iPhone that I use every day. I rarely write anything on paper. And I would feel like an idiot writing something on a yellow pad and handing it to my Admin and asking her to type it up for me. It's just easier for me to do it myself. So I peck away at the keyboard. If I had known what was up ahead, I would have ignored my pastor's advice and signed up for that typing class!

Though typewriters are out, knowing how to type has become an indispensible part of most people's lives today. But what about abstinence? Is that something that's just part of the past? Many people would tell you that's the case. But I want to challenge you to think carefully about this issue before you just dismiss it based on someone else's advice. Our perspective, like that old pastor of mine, is limited. But God's isn't. Sex is a Wonderful Thing, but…

At this point in your life you may have already faced times when you had the opportunity to abandon sexual restraint for sexual indulgence. If you haven't faced this yet, chances are extremely high that sometime in the near future you'll be tempted to have sex. Whether it's with someone you really like or just hooking up, the opportunity is most likely going to come your way.

King Solomon and his bride-to-be stand out in the Bible as a couple who waited to have sex, even when they were engaged to be married. Waiting wasn't easy for them, just like it probably won't be for you. Several times in Song of Solomon, the book that tells us their love story, they use the phrase, "Do not arouse or awaken love until it so desires." That's the poetic way of saying, "We've made a commitment to wait until marriage to have sex. It's not going to be easy, but we're going to wait."

So they held off on sex. They refused to give in to what their bodies wanted to do. They intentionally kept themselves out of places and situations that would have made it easy to give in.

Sex is a wonderful thing. God's big on it. It was His idea! He designed it not only to populate the world, but also for our pleasure. But He's also very clear that it was created for within marriage.

Much can be said about the "why" of this clear biblical standard, but for this chapter I'd urge you to consider an old-fashioned abstinence commitment in light of 1 Peter 2:11. There Peter writes, "Dear friends, I urge you, as aliens and strangers in the world, to *abstain* from sinful desires, which war against your soul" (1 Peter 2:11).

Here you find Peter giving his friends some advice about sex in a world much like ours where giving in to the desires of the flesh was considered a natural and recreational activity, especially when it came to sexual indulgence. Contrary to society's popular opinion, he urged his fellow Christ-following friends to make the same commitment Solomon and his fiancé had made. To hold themselves back from giving in to sinful sex and to save sex for marriage.

Living With Your Sexual Desires

Odds are you have sexual desires. If you're a guy, you probably can't get through a day without thinking about sex. You know from first-hand experience that sexual desire is in you. God is asking you to control those desires by making a commitment to abstain.

Abstinence (*ab-sti-nence*—noun: the fact or practice of restraining oneself from indulging in something) gets a bad rap though it really can be a good thing. Take eating for instance. We think about food a lot. Numerous times each day. As human beings we need food. We want food. We crave food. In fact, just thinking about it while I'm writing this paragraph is making me hungry!

Eating is a good thing. We need to eat. But if we can't control those desires and we eat something every time we find ourselves craving something, the end result is not going to be pretty. It will only be a matter of time before we're fat and really unhealthy. Call it a good desire gone bad. Without self-regulation and appropriate abstinence related to food, our bodies would be in serious trouble. Abstinence really can be a good thing. Our health demands it when it comes to food. So we spend our entire life trying to control those cravings for ice cream or donuts or whatever your splurge of choice is so we can live a long healthy life. The trade off is worth it.

In it's own important and similar way, you must also regulate your sexual desires to keep your soul from being damaged. Does the possibility of you damaging your soul concern you? It should. That's why Peter makes it the singular point of focus when he pleads with his friends to abstain from fulfilling sinful desires, which would include sex outside of marriage. Even with someone you know, care about, and perhaps are even engaged to be married to. God says that sex inside of marriage is a great thing, but sex outside of marriage will damage your soul.

Not Easy But Definitely Worth It

Holding yourself back from what your body craves isn't easy. Peter uses battle terminology in describing what you can expect. Abstaining from sex will be like fighting a war. Constant vigilance is required if you hope to come out on the winning side. The world, the devil, and your own flesh will wage a vicious battle for your soul, the core of your being. And one of the easiest weapons to use against you is sex. A natural desire (which in itself isn't sin!) that can easily get way out of control. And a death blow to your soul is a death blow to your very being.

When Peter spoke of the soul, he had in mind the real you. The part of you that encompasses your mind, spirit, heart, and emotions. That person deep inside that is you. If you've been hurt —really hurt—by someone, you know what it's like to feel the pain all the way deep inside you, to the core of your being. The Bible is telling us that wounds from sexual sin go all the way to your very soul. No wonder Peter urged his friends to abstain from giving in to their sinful sexual desires.

The fact is that sex is much more than a physical act. It's not just a fun recreational activity. It's so much more than that. It reaches deep into the core of your soul. When it's within marriage, with someone you've committed yourself to for life, it creates a unique bond between the two of you that no one else will share. But when it's outside of marriage, it wounds your soul like nothing else can. Paul touched on this same matter when he wrote to the believers living in promiscuous Corinth. He said, "Flee from sexual immorality. All other sins a man commits are outside his body, but he who sins sexually sins against his own body" (1 Corinthians 6:18). Like Peter, Paul pleaded with believers to abstain from sexual immorality because of the damage it would do to their souls.

Erwin McManus, in his book *Soul Cravings,* insightfully says this:

> "There is no such thing as free sex. It always comes at a cost. With it you either give your heart, or you give your soul. It seems you can have sex without giving love, but you can't have sex without giving a part of yourself… When sex is an act of love, it is a gift. When sex is a substitute for love, it is a trap…we are pillaging our souls."

Sex outside of marriage pillages the soul. It strikes a death blow to the core of your being. Take it from this college student who found that out the hard way.

> *When I was in the seventh grade I made a commitment to save sex for marriage and had even been preaching it to my friends and anyone else who would listen to me. I stayed true to my word for almost 7 years.*
>
> *But then I met a guy through a friend. We spent a lot of time together and forged what I thought was a very strong and true bond. He said he loved me and I believed it. He knew that I was a virgin and had intended on staying that way until I was married. I had told him how important it was to me since it was 'the only thing I had not messed up yet.'*
>
> *Nevertheless, one night things started getting heavy and I went along with it. We'd talked about being together forever and I just felt so comfortable with him. I lost my virginity that night. We had sex again a few more times until I put an end to it, saying that I didn't want to get too attached to him only to be disappointed. We stopped seeing each other about a month after that night. And a month after that, I found out everything was a lie. I've never felt so much emotion at one time in my life. It was the most horrid combination of unimaginable humiliation, betrayal and emptiness.*

I could have said no. I could have put an end to the night long before it progressed the way it did. If I could go back in time, I would never have put myself in that bedroom. I would have never let myself be that vulnerable with someone who did not have God's blessing in my life. I wish with all my heart that I had stayed true to my commitment.

But it is impossible to go back in time. All I can do now is continue the healing process with God's help. I hope with everything in me that my friends who have stayed pure to this point will continue to do so until they say, 'I do.' We all make mistakes in life but that is one mistake we don't have to make."

O how I wish this college student had kept her abstinence commitment. For her sake. But at the same time, I'm thankful that she now understands even more how important a commitment to abstinence is.

According to popular opinion, abstinence is old fashioned and out of date. But according to God, abstinence is an important way to protect your soul from serious damage. I hope that will make waiting for sex until marriage worth it for you, even at those times when everything within you may be saying to give in. Don't!

To those readers who have already had sex:
Our God is a God of grace and fresh starts. If you have already given in to sexual temptation, you can choose to live by a different standard from here on. God promises to forgive us and cleanse us. His grace can help you have a fresh start today.

Old-fashioned and out-of-date?

Satan would love nothing more than to inflict a death blow on your soul. Let these verses encourage you to vigilantly stand firm against his devious destructive ways.

How do the following passages confirm that sex outside of marriage is sin?

Hebrews 13:4 – Marriage should be honored by all, and the marriage bed kept pure, for God will judge the adulterer and all the sexually immoral.

1 Thessalonians 4:3 – It is God's will that you should be sanctified: that you should avoid sexual immorality.

Ephesians 5:3 – But among you there must not be even a hint of sexual immorality, or of any kind of impurity, or of greed, because these are improper for God's holy people.

Colossians 3:5 – Put to death, therefore, whatever belongs to your earthly nature: sexual immorality, impurity, lust, evil desires and greed, which is idolatry.

Carefully consider each word Peter uses to urge his friends to resist sinful pleasures. How can what he says help you live a life of sexual abstinence?

1 Peter 2:11 – Dear friends, I urge you, as aliens and strangers in the world, to abstain from sinful desires, which war against your soul.

In light of what Paul says in the following verse, what specific ways can you flee sexual immorality?

1 Corinthians 6:18 – Flee from sexual immorality. All other sins a man commits are outside his body, but he who sins sexually sins against his own body.

twenty-one

Pornography
Playing with fire

OUR THREE CHILDREN grew up twelve miles from the world famous beaches of Malibu, California. If you've been to the West Coast—or seen movies or car commercials or TMZ star sightings—you know how gorgeous Malibu is. And I'm not just talking about the sunbathers soaking up the rays. Malibu is just one of some really beautiful beaches along the left coast.

Take a road trip up PCH (Pacific Coast Highway 1) sometime and see if you don't agree—the beaches along the Pacific Ocean are stunning. That's why we as a family would climb into our minivan and drive over to Malibu as often as we could. Even if it was just to set a beach chair in the sand, breath in the salty air, and watch the sun set over the ocean. The sound of waves crashing against the sand can pull you away from the worries and problems you'll be driving back to when you leave. There's just something calming and peaceful about the ocean.

But... for those of you who have also spent a lot of time along the Southern California coast, you know that it isn't all a glimpse of heaven. Along with our Gudgel family memories of good times at the beach in Malibu, we've got our share of "not so much fun" memories too.

One of our worst days on the beach began like any other. After we poured out of the van and grabbed the chairs and towels and boogie boards and ice chests and sunscreen and all the other stuff you need for a day at the beach, we headed out to "our spot" near Life Guard station #11 at Zuma Beach. Like a student sits in the same unassigned seat in a class, we repeatedly returned to this beach spot because it was usually a safe place to swim and hang out with friends who met at this location. And it was nice having a lifeguard station nearby. Call it a security blanket, parental wisdom, or a providential premonition, the day our oldest son, Brent, got caught in a riptide we were glad for the location we chose.

A riptide spells danger. Get caught in one and you could drown. Even if you're a super star athlete. That's what happened to Rhainnon Hull. She was a world class runner whose strength, speed, focus, coordination, control, and resolve were no match for a riptide that sucked her out to her death along the Pacific Coast of Costa Rica.

Lifeguards can look out over the ocean and see when a riptide is forming. And when they see one at Zuma they immediately get everyone out of the water along that part of the beach. A Red Flag is posted on the closest lifeguard tower and the width of the riptide is marked off with two flags placed along the shore. When you see those three flags flying, everyone knows to stay out of the water in that area.

People who hang out a lot at SoCal beaches also know that if you happen to be out in the water when a riptide forms, before the flags have been posted, your best chance of getting out alive is to stay calm and either (1) swim *parallel* to the shoreline until you're out of the dangerous current and able to then swim to shore or (2) to float passively allowing the riptide to drag you out past it's current at which point you should be able to swim around it and back to shore. If you try to fight the current by trying to take the fastest route to shore, you could eventually tire from exhaustion and drown like Hull tragically did.

Knowing what to do when you're caught in a riptide can save your life, but if you panic and forget, or like our son Brent you get caught in it without even realizing what's going on, your death could be imminent. Fortunately for Brent and us, while we were all just enjoying our day at the beach, the lifeguard at station #11 that day saw what was happening, grabbed his rescue board, and made a beeline for our son.

Our second clue that something was wrong was when the lifeguard started yelling to Brent and told him to start swimming parallel to the beach instead of trying to swim in to shore. Brent, who was 11 at the time, had no idea why he should do that and was confused. All he knew was that he wanted to get to shore but for some reason he wasn't making any progress!

The lifeguard saw what Brent didn't. He was attempting to swim back to shore against a riptide and that's why he wasn't getting anywhere even though he kept trying and trying. If he kept that up he would eventually get too tired and could drown. But the lifeguard wasn't going to let that happen.

As the lifeguard jumped into the water and started swimming toward Brent he yelled, "You're caught in a riptide. Stop trying to swim to shore." Fortunately for all of us a few seconds after that the lifeguard reached Brent and helped him get safely back to shore. Ever since that day we've all been very aware of how dangerous riptides can be and we know what to do if we ever get stuck in one.

Caught in a Pornographic Riptide

Pornography is like a riptide. You may already know that by experience. I hope not, but if you're among the 70% of men or 21% of women that struggle with porn, you're in trouble and possibly headed for disaster, whether you know it or not.

On any given day 40 million Americans view porn, many without any idea of how dangerous it is. They think they're just sailing along when they're actually being dragged into something that could destroy them. Like a riptide, and like most sinful behavior, it may even feel and seem right, but the fact is you are being sucked toward death.

Your appetite for porn will grow exponentially. It may start out as something small and simple and "just checking it out" but it won't stop there. You'll want more. You'll need more, because soon what you started with isn't enough. The addictive pull is predictable. Viewing porn creates a powerful inner desire for more. Your need for emotional and physical gratification escalates. Soft porn is exchanged for hard porn. Mild images are replaced with explicit images. The sensual is traded for the violent. What begins as "just for fun," becomes a relentless, overwhelming sexual compulsion.

I've seen this sexual riptide effect firsthand, fortunately not in my own life, but in the lives of others I've helped rescue. Back before the internet made access to porn so easy, one individual took me to his home to show me a bedroom closet stacked wall-to-wall, three feet high with Playboy magazines. "I need you to help me stop," he said. "I'm addicted to pornography. I've tried to stop so many times, but so far I haven't been able to."

Tragically, this is the norm for people who get sucked into porn: compulsive addiction, lies, fantasizing, guilt, confession, broken promises, …stuck in the grip of sin.

Pornographic Riptides Can Kill You

It's no wonder Solomon told a naïve young man, "Don't lustfully fantasize on her beauty, nor be taken in by her bedroom eyes…Can you build a fire in your lap and not burn your pants?" (Proverbs 6:25,27, MSG). The obvious answer—NO. You may think it's just harmless fun. Just entertainment. But your story is still being written. With every quick glance at a picture, every return visit to that website that feeds your lust, you're adding another stick to a growing fire that is going to hurt you in the end. Is that really what you want?

Jesus set the bar high when He said, "…Don't think you've preserved your virtue simply by staying out of bed. Your *heart* can be corrupted by lust even quicker than your *body*. Those leering looks you think nobody notices—they also corrupt. Let's not pretend this is easier than it really is. If you want to live a morally pure life, here's what you have to do: You have to blind your right eye the moment you catch it in a lustful leer. You have to choose

to live one-eyed or else be dumped on a moral trash pile."
(Matthew 5:27b-29).

Sounds drastic, doesn't it. Rip out your eye? Seriously? Thankfully
that's not literally what Jesus meant or we'd all be blind in no time.
Jesus was speaking figuratively. Do whatever you have to do to get
your eyes off what's wrong and onto what's right. Now!

Drastic Action Required

Is the computer the primary source of lust in your life? Are you
having a sexual relationship in your mind with whatever or
whoever you're looking at on your computer? Stop justifying and
rationalizing what you are doing and decide right now to do
whatever it takes to put pornography behind you once and for all.
If that requires drastic action, take it. I'd like to say get rid of your
computer, but we know that's not going to happen in today's
world. But you can take steps to safeguard yourself from ever
looking at another porn site. Here are a few minimum actions I'd
urge you to take:

1. Begin by confessing your sin to God and a trusted
   friend, counselor, or pastor. This vital first step is
   absolutely necessary in breaking out of the stronghold
   that pornography has on your life.

2. Commit to only use your computer in public places.
   Don't use it in a room that can be locked.

3. When working on your computer, have the computer
   screen face out toward others. Knowing that others
   can see what you are looking at can be a helpful
   deterrent.

4. Only use your computer when others are around. As
   much as possible, work on your computer when
   others are in the same room or close by.

5. Make yourself accountable. Begin by loading
   pornographic filtering software onto your computer.
   Then ask a few trusted people to keep you
   accountable. Use a tool like x3watch (www.x3watch.com)
   that will monitor and screen what you look at online.

It will also notify your accountability partners of questionable websites you go to.

Sounds drastic? Perhaps. But if you're serious about honoring God with your body, soul, mind, and spirit—with all that you are—you need to seriously safeguard yourself from pornography. Stop playing with fire before you get burned or add more damage to what has already been damaged.

Get Out Now

I have a friend who secretly struggled with pornography since Middle School. As a Christ-follower he lived in a constant state of guilt and shame because he couldn't get out of the death grip porn had on his life. After he got married he thought his addiction to porn would go away. It didn't. It kept coming back. It kept teasing him and promising to give him something better than what he had with his wife. It never did. He was miserable.

A few years ago my friend found a way out. Finally in a state of desperation he confessed his pornographic addiction to another pastor and then to me. Healing begins with confession. That simple yet courageous action didn't all-of-a-sudden fix him, but it did set him on a path toward transformational change.

His life to this day is continuing to change through the work of God, the Word of God, and people of God. The destructive fires that once were burning him have died down. He's no longer stuck in a sexual riptide. He's finding freedom from pornography and his life is better for it. Danger still lurks all around him, but he's learned how to stay out of its deadly current. You can too.

Playing with fire

Now's the time to commit or recommit yourself to a porn free life. Let the following questions help you steer clear of porn's deadly grip.

Does pornography have a grip on you? Honestly answer the following questions. If you're afraid someone may see your answers, write them down in code!

- *Do you regularly look at pornographic magazines, movies, or websites?*

- *Do you look forward to or plan the next time you will look at porn?*

- *Do you lie about or hide what you look at on the web?*

- *Have you vowed to stop looking at certain sites only to give in the next time temptation arises?*

- *Do you masturbate while doing any of the above?*

In addition to the two Bible passages discussed in this chapter (Prov 6:25,27; Matt 5:27b-29) **how can the following passages also help you do what's best?**

1 Peter 2:11 – Dear friends, I urge you, as aliens and strangers in the world, to abstain from sinful desires, which war against your soul.

1 Corinthians 6:12 – I can do anything I want to if Christ has not said no, but some of these things aren't good for me. Even if I am allowed to do them, I'll refuse to if I think they might get such a grip on me that I can't easily stop when I want to. (TLB)

What practical steps can you take from here on to keep yourself away from pornography's death grip?

PART EIGHT

PAINFUL EXPERIENCES

twenty-two

Fear
When bad stuff happens

THURSDAY NIGHT, November 13, 2008. Westmont College freshman Megan Reed planned to celebrate her 19th birthday at a popular Italian restaurant on Santa Barbara's State Street. But Megan and her friends' best laid birthday plans never materialized. Instead, they spent the night in Murchison Gymnasium—with over 800 fellow students, faculty, staff, preview students, and neighbors —sheltered from the fast moving flames of a wildfire that ultimately burned 1,900 acres and destroyed 210 homes in Santa Barbara County. Call it an unplanned, unwanted, unpaid for educational experience. For some it would be the most life changing experience in their college years.

What started out as just another laidback Thursday evening dinner took an unexpected turn from food to fear when flames were spotted on the Montecito mountainside and the evacuation alarm sounded. Students enjoying their all-you-can-eat meal in the dining commons jumped up and left their dinner behind; others hanging out in their dorms or the library rushed to find somewhere safely away from the approaching flames; students outside having fun with Frisbees and soccer balls hightailed it down the nearby asphalt pathway to the gym.

As far as evacuations go, everything worked perfectly, just as planned and practiced. Westmont resides in the beautiful hills of Montecito on a gorgeous 110 acre campus with lush gardens and trees. When all is well, it's a beautiful setting for an education. But in the path of a brushfire, it can be a nightmare. That's why several years earlier they realized it was necessary to set in place an evacuation plan.

Rather than trying to get 1,300 students, plus professors and staff, off the campus and risk a fire overtaking them while driving down the highly flammable eucalyptus tree lined Montecito streets, Murchison Gym was selected as the safest place to evacuate to due to its location and sturdy cinder block construction. Not only for those at Westmont, but also for the surrounding community.

In anticipation of that possibility the American Red Cross had stocked the gym with blankets and pillows. That Thursday night the gym was filled with hundreds of anxiety filled evacuees who were thankful for the prior planning. The air in the gym was sticky and smoky, but the conditions inside were much better than what was going on outside where smoke from the raging fire was filling the campus and the surrounding neighborhoods. Trees ignited, buildings burned, even lawns were torched as the untamed fire took out everything in its path.

People stood, paced, sat, and sprawled out in the gym as they waited and tried their best not to freak out. Many formed circles and prayed. Some sang. Megan remembers telling herself to "just keep breathing…but not too deeply."

The worst of the fire blew past them sometime after midnight, but not before it had left devastating loss in its wake. The fire destroyed the homes of sixteen Westmont faculty members and nine Westmont structures including four of the seventeen Clark Hall dorms, the Physics Lab, the Psychology Building, the Math Building, plus two Quonset huts. It was the worst fire to hit the Westmont Montecito campus in its sixty-three year history.

Around 2:00 am those who found refuge in the smoky gym were given the okay to relocate to San Marcos High School in Santa

Barbara or to Reality Church in Carpinteria. Never did a breathe of fresh air taste so good. It's a miracle no one died in what is now known as the Tea Fire of 2008.

Times of fear and loss change you. They're often unexpected and totally out of your control. And whether it's a big deal or something small, when the dust settles and you pick up the pieces and try to go on, you're different because of the experience. Students like Megan who went through the Tea Fire came out of it different.

In the midst of those times of fear and loss, the promise found in Isaiah 43:2 rings true: "When you pass through the waters, I will be with you; and when you pass through the rivers, they will not sweep over you. When you walk through the fire, you will not be burned; the flames will not set you ablaze."

For Megan that promise, first given to the nation of Judah, became more than a few nice words on a page. It is now indelibly etched into her life and her beliefs due to her firsthand firestorm experience. Let's take a closer look at this comforting promise, first made to the nation of Judah, because it reveals two facts that can help you make it through your own times of fear and loss.

When You Pass Through

We have to accept the fact that life in this fallen world includes fear and loss… like devastating firestorms. You may wish this wasn't true but the fact is, if you have a pulse you'll have problems. There will be times when bad things happen that are totally out of your control. And your life will change because of it. As much as we would like to eliminate pain, hurt, loss, disease, and the like from life, there will always be another problem ahead to endure.

It's not accidental that God used the word *when* three times in this verse. He didn't say *if*. He said *when*. *When* you pass through troubled waters; *when* you pass through torrential rivers; *when* you're overtaken by a devastating firestorm.

The intensity of these difficult times will vary greatly. Sometimes the water will be a little troubled. Sometimes the river will be raging and flooding. Sometimes the problem will be like a devastating firestorm sweeping through and destroying everything in its path.

Recently my oldest son Brent and his wife Danielle were sharing with me some of the hard times they experienced while in college. "Dad, I can still remember getting a call from a friend who was planning on being my roommate. He and I had signed a lease on an apartment that we were excited to live in during our junior year in college. I thought everything was set until the last minute when he bailed out on our agreement and left me to pay for the apartment alone. That was really hard to take."

Danielle chimed in, "The girls at our college were repeatedly hit with similar feelings when a guy walked into our life, only to eventually bail on the relationship. That was tough to take, especially at our college where girls outnumbered guys two to one!"

"For me," Brent added, "the greatest loss I went though was when Andrea died. I'll never forget her. She was really special. She had a great relationship with God. I had the privilege of filming her for a week while she was in Mexico ministering to the poor. The video we made of her and her ministry encouraged others to follow in her selfless example. A year after we made that video she died in a car accident. I ended up doing a second video that was shown at her memorial service. That was a hard time for me, and our entire student body."

So was the tragedy of 9/11 that hit our world while they were both in college. Anyone who lived through that devastating event, whether first hand or simply watching on television, was indelibly changed by the merciless Al-Qaeda attacks on our nation. A really bad situation that was totally out of our control. Fear. Loss.

When you pass through. Fear, hurt, pain, and loss is simply the way life is. Which is why we so desperately need to hang onto a second key fact found in Isaiah 43:2 where the Lord makes this promise, *I will be with you.*

I Will Be With You
Thank God. Whatever trouble comes your way, you have God's

guarantee – He will be with you. No matter what. That's not just a nice thought, it's an amazing fact. God will be *with* you just like He was *with* King David, whom we read about in the Old Testament.

When David was facing hard times—and he faced a lot of them!—he would think about this promise, which is actually the most repeated promise found in the Bible. In one of the most familiar Psalms found in the Bible, he said, "Even though I walk through the valley of the shadow of death, I will fear no evil, for *you are with me*…"(Psalm 23:6). Knowing that the Lord was *with* David gave him courage in the face of fear. When David remembered that incredible fact that God was *with* him, it gave him the perspective he needed to endure the circumstance he faced.

When times of fear and loss come your way, knowing the Lord is with you can be the difference between panic and peace.

A year ago I took Camden, my three-year old grandson, out on a Wave Runner on Flat Head Lake (the biggest lake west of the Great Lakes) in Montana. The ride started out great but ended with unexpected trouble. Even at three, Cam loves to go fast, which we were doing. Until the Wave Runner stopped. I tried to get it started again, but no such luck. We were stuck.

There were two more wave runners and a boat back at the house, so someone could have easily come to get us…if I hadn't forgotten to bring my cell phone along. So we floated for a long time until we finally drifted over to someone's boat dock. We walked up to the house and fortunately found someone at home. A nice man drove us back to the home we were staying in and we took the boat out to tow back the stranded wave runner.

Camden, at three years old, saw the whole thing as a great adventure. To him, running out of gas on a lake without a cell phone or anyone else around was no cause for fear. Because he was *with* his grandpa. But it would have been a completely different story if he had been out there all alone.

When you leave home, you are going to face a bunch of situations that can easily put you into a state of fear or panic. Things are going to happen that aren't good. Things that are out of your control. It's just life. And one of the best things you can do when life doesn't go as planned is to check your perspective. What do you see?

GODISNOWHERE

Hopefully you won't end up saying God-is-nowhere, but instead find encouragement, hope, and strength in the fact that God-is-now-here. Always has been, always will be. Remembering that will give you the hope you need when you need it most.

When bad stuff happens

Knowing God is with you will make all the difference in a world filled with the consequences of sin.

Can you think of a time in your life when someone's presence with you made the difference between "panic" and "peace"?

In what ways does knowing God will be *with* you give you hope for whatever lies ahead?

Take some time and commit to memory one of the following versions of Isaiah 43:2. Doing so may be a big help to you, just when you need it most.

Isaiah 43:2 – When you pass through the waters, I will be with you; and when you pass through the rivers, they will not sweep over you. When you walk through the fire, you will not be burned; the flames will not set you ablaze. (NIV)

Isaiah 43:2 – When you pass through waters, I will be with you. When you cross rivers, you will not drown. When you walk through fire, you will not be burned, nor will the flames hurt you. (NCV)

twenty-three

Failure

Try to fail forward

THE PURPOSE OF this chapter is to hopefully keep you from failing after you fail. And if you're thinking that you can skip this chapter because you don't plan to fail, I'd encourage you to think again. The odds of anyone, including you, avoiding failure on their way to success are not good. Even the great ones failed.

They Failed, But Didn't Fail

For all those famous people we hear about who have done great things, more often than not, their success came after failure. A brief history lesson on some people you've probably heard of:

> **Walt Disney:** Disneyland or Disneyworld—*the happiest place on earth.* But know this, neither park would be there had Mr. Disney given up when he failed to make it as a newspaper editor. Hard to believe that he was fired because "he lacked imagination and had no good ideas." He didn't fail after he failed.
>
> **Steven Spielberg:** He's become an icon because of the films he's directed: Indiana Jones, ET, Hook, Jurassic Park, War Horse, Saving Private Ryan, Schindler's List...

This three time Academy Award winning Director was rejected three times as an applicant at USC's School of Theater, Film and Television. He hasn't failed after he failed.

J.K. Rowling: Before publishing her first novel she saw herself as the "biggest failure she knew." She was nearly penniless and dependant on welfare, divorced, trying to raise a child on her own, and severely depressed. Her first Harry Potter book was rejected by the first twelve publishers she submitted the manuscript to. Finally, a small publishing house in London agreed to publish her book even though the chief editor told her she should get a day job because she had little chance of making it in children's books. Well J.R. no longer needs a day job having sold 400 million Harry Potter books. She hasn't failed after she failed.

Michael Jordan: He's a basketball legend now. But did you know that he was cut from his High School basketball team because he wasn't good enough. That didn't stop him from making it in the NBA. But even then he experienced a series of failures and successes. Jordan said, "I have missed more than 9,000 shots in my career. I have lost almost 300 games. On 26 occasions I have been entrusted to take the game winning shot, and I missed. I have failed over and over and over again in my life. And that is why I succeed." He didn't fail after he failed.

It's been said that most people give up just when they're about to achieve success. They quit on the one-yard line. They give up at the last minute of the game, one foot from a winning touch down. That certainly wasn't the case with the great ones listed above. Failure did not deter them from pursuing what they longed for. Along the way they failed—but they didn't fail.

The Wall of Failures
Even our examples of great men of faith in the Bible failed along the way to the legacy we know today. Abraham and Moses and

David and Solomon are just a few of many in the Old Testament. All great men who experienced significant failure.

Then in the New Testament, look at Simon Peter, the disciple of Jesus who was the strong natural leader among the twelve. A guy who ended up making a major impact in the first century, and that impact continues to influence the world today. Thousands of people became Christ followers because of his fearless ministry. But take note - his greatest impact came *after* his *before* story. And his *before* story was often a major FAIL.

Peter's most notorious failure came one night when a little girl asked him the simple question, "Aren't you one of the guys who was following Jesus?" You'd think a question like that wouldn't trip him up. After all, Peter gave up his fishing business to follow Jesus and then he spent three+ years living life with Him. He had adamantly declared he'd never ever turn his back on Jesus. But when Jesus' life was on the line, and possibly Peter's too, he flat-out denied he was a Christ follower. Not just once, but three times. He swore he did not know that man!

Major FAIL. No denying it. He failed Jesus big time. And then he ran off and cried like a baby after letting the Lord down. But fortunately for Peter his failure wasn't the end of the story. Jesus made sure of that. Peter definitely failed, but he didn't fail.

You'll also find Paul's photo on the Wall of Failures next to Peter's. For years, when he was known as Saul, he focused on taking Jesus and His followers down. He wanted nothing to do with the Rabbi who claimed he was the Messiah. Saul was a devout Jew and he couldn't let this Jesus get away with claiming to be God. He saw Jesus as someone who had to be stopped and it was his job to do just that.

But then Saul had an unexpected encounter with Jesus and from then on he was never the same. His entire life, including his name, was changed…for good! No longer bent on destroying Christianity, Paul made a 180 degree turn and began living his life as strongly *for* Christ as he had *against* Him. His commitment to preach the Gospel and live differently was amazing.

But even though he was sold out to Jesus, he too failed time and time again. He longed to be a better person than he was. On one occasion in a moment of candor and complete frustration he said: "I don't really understand myself, for I want to do what is right, but I don't do it. Instead, I do what I hate." (Romans 7:15)

Ever felt like that? Ever said something similar? *I know what I need to do. Why can't I just get my act together and do it?! I keep trying to do the right thing, but I keep failing.* There you have it. Failure in a nutshell. The inability to do what you know needs to be done. It happens to the best of us.

The normal Christian life is often cyclical: success, followed by failure, followed by success, then another failure, then more success… Unfortunately, as long as we're in this present world, that's going to be the norm. It's the way life is for now. Actor Mickey Rooney got it right when he said, "You always pass failure on your way to success."

How to Succeed After You Fail

And what about you? When people look back at your life what will they see, hear, or tell? A lot will depend on how you respond now when you fail. A key determining factor will be whether or not you fail forward. If that happens, you'll discover that your failures aren't fatal but can actually become stepping stones to success. So here's what I would suggest you keep in mind the next time failure comes your way.

First, LOOK UP. Motivational speaker Les Brown says, "When you are down on your back, if you can look up, you can get up." Of course I believe that because I believe in God. Become like King David who said, "I lift up my eyes to the hills—where does my help come from? My help comes from the LORD, the Maker of heaven and earth (Psalm 121:2)." Lift up your eyes. Look all around you at creation. See how incredibly awesome and amazing it is. Look at what God made. Know that the God who made it can make anything. Anything!

Whenever you feel like a failure—especially when you actually have failed—look up. Look up to the one who gives us hope. The one who doesn't give up on us. The one who can lead us out of our failures and into success. The God who sees, knows, cares, heals, leads, and provides for all that we need. When down, look up!

Then LISTEN UP! Often it's through failure that we learn our best lessons. Thomas Edison was a great inventor. He made the incandescent light bulb. Where would we be without light bulbs? But that's his *after* story. Did you know that his success in finding the right element for an incandescent light bulb did not come until after 200 previous attempts. That's his *before* story. And when questioned about his repeated failures he said, "Don't call it a failure, call it an education. I know 200 ways that don't work."

I love that. That's definitely putting a positive spin on failure. But it's also true. Being down does not mean you're out. Failure can be your greatest teacher if you learn from your mistakes and shortcomings. Like H. Stanley Judd said, "Learn from your failures and go on to the next challenge. It's okay to fail. If you're not failing, you're not growing." Before you get up, pick up something that will keep you from making the same mistake again.

So I'd urge you to LOOK UP, LISTEN UP, and then GET UP and KEEP GOING! Time isn't going to stop and wait for you. There's a good chance your FAIL is just a step along the way to success. So pick yourself up and keep moving.

Now I do need to add that there may be times when your FAIL is telling you it's the end of the line. There may be times when the best thing you can do is admit, "I'm just not cut out for this. God made me a circle and this requires a square." But think carefully before you give up.

If what you're trying to do doesn't match up with who you are, with your unique talents and abilities, then get up and *go on to something else*. But if you really feel you're headed in the right direction, please don't make a bigger mistake by giving up after your failure.

According to Dr. Paul Meyer, "Ninety percent of all who fail are not actually defeated. They simply quit." If it's true that most people achieve their greatest success one step beyond what looks like their greatest failure, let that person be you. Join with Albert Einstein who said, "It's not that I'm so smart, it's just that I stay with problems longer." Be that kind of person. The ones who don't give up, even when they fail. Like the Proverb says, *Though a righteous man falls seven times, he rises again* (Proverbs 24:16a). With God's guidance, empowerment, encouragement, and wisdom, your best days can be the days that follow apparent failure.

So Get Up and Keep Going

Harland David Sanders came up with a recipe for fried chicken that he thought was good. Really good. But he faced rejection 1,008 times before someone else agreed. And now millions of people who eat at KFC agree.

The manuscript for *Carrie* was rejected by publishers thirty times. The author was so frustrated that he threw it away. But his wife literally got it out of the trash and urged him to resubmit it, one more time. And that's how Steven King became one of the best-selling authors of all time. He didn't fail after he failed, thanks to his wife!

The chances of you failing are high, but that doesn't mean you should give up. In fact, the best thing you can do is learn from your failures, and get up and keep going. Learn to fail without failing.

Try to fail forward

Knowing that your failures do not make you a failure can make a huge difference in how you view your life and circumstances. And in your future! Take a few minutes to reflect on how you're doing in this area.

How have you failed in the past? How did you react to that failure?

What potential failures do you see in your future?

How can the concepts of: Look up, Listen up, Get up and keep going, help you fail without failing?

How are the following verses helpful or encouraging to you?

Proverbs 24:16a – For though a righteous man falls seven times, he rises again.

Galatians 6:9 – Let us not become weary in doing good, for at the proper time we will reap a harvest if we do not give up.

Philippians 3:13 – No, dear brothers and sisters, I have not achieved it, but I focus on this one thing: Forgetting the past and looking forward to what lies ahead... (NLT)

Isaiah 42:3a – A bruised reed he will not break, and a smoldering wick he will not snuff out.

twenty-four

Grief

Let yourself cry and ask why

I'D LIKE TO ASK Adam and Eve, the first man and woman, a question. Just one question. I'd like to ask them the same question my mother asked me after I did something stupid. You know the question; you've probably asked it of someone or remember someone asking it of you. It's a simple question. Just four words. Here it is: *What were you thinking?* That's not asking Mr. and Mrs. Adam and Eve too much is it? *What were you thinking?*

I know I am supposed to be respectful of my ancestors and all, but come on. Their decision to eat fruit off the forbidden tree was stupid. It was the only thing God had asked them not to do! Really dumb. And if they'd like me to elaborate on my question I'd say: *Did you think that God was just kidding around when He said, 'In the day you eat of it you will surely DIE?'*

Look around. We have plenty of proof that the Lord wasn't kidding when He warned the first man and woman of the consequences of disobedience. Thanks to their foolish decision, we live in a world filled with the hurtful consequences of sin: death, suffering, sorrow, crying…the list is long and painful. We hurt and are hurt and wish life wasn't like it is. We long to live in a world without pain, or suffering, or tears, or sorrow, or death.

When Life Doesn't Turn Out Like It Should

Three months ago I saw how dreadful pain can be as I attended the memorial service for a twenty-five year old who had died suddenly. Everyone was grieving. The father and mother, brother, aunts, uncles, friends, friends of friends, church members and attenders. Everyone. More than 1000 people came to the Memorial Service. Everywhere you looked people were hurting in the painful aftermath of an unplanned, unexpected death of a really likeable guy.

Unfortunately, I've attended a lot of funerals—they come with pastoral ministry. But this twenty-something's death really got me thinking. Solomon's words came to mind from Ecclesiastes 7:2 when he said, "It is better to go to a house of mourning than to go to a house of feasting, for death is the destiny of every man; the living should take this to heart." Like a wake-up call at a hotel, this young man's death, amidst the sorrow and regret, got a lot of people thinking about the seriousness of life and death and asking questions like he did.

His parents spoke at the service. Never before had I heard two parents at the passing of a son say the things they said. Their love for their son was obvious. Their deepest regret was the loss of his future and his potential impact on the world. Had it not been that he had received Jesus as his Savior as a young child, they would have been in even worse shape. They chose to find solace in the hope that if anyone comes to the Lord in childlike faith, he has passed from death to life.

During his childhood and teen years his love for the Lord showed. He wanted to live for Jesus and did. But in high school he began to struggle with unanswered questions like: "If there is a God, why doesn't He intervene and eliminate suffering and pain?" His search for satisfactory answers to his questions intensified when three friends died in the last half of his senior year. One died in January, the second in February, the third in March. Their deaths put him in a spiritual tailspin.

Unanswered Questions

At the memorial service, his uncle gave the eulogy message. He spoke of him as if he was his own son. He loved him dearly and had spent significant time with him. They had tons of outdoor fun together biking, surfing, hiking, and mountain climbing. He said they also frequently talked about spiritual things. "Recently," he said, "we had one of our many conversations about questions he had about life and God. He peppered me with a series of 'why' questions: Why do innocent people suffer? Why did God let my friends die? Why is the world falling apart?" His uncle said he wasn't able to answer all of his questions, which was something he lamented. "But then again," he said, "this side of heaven, no one may be able to give definitive answers to questions like these in this life."

In the aftermath of this young man's death, it would be natural for his parents to be undone by their own unanswered questions. Why our son? Why did he have to die so young? Why now? What happened? How did he die? Was he saved for sure? Will he be in heaven when we get there? Could we have done more to help him with his doubts? Where did we as parents go wrong? What should or could we have done different?"

As his parents and uncle spoke at the memorial service, they pleaded with those who had questions to "Be like our son and ask your questions about life and death and spiritual matters. Have the same courage he did to ask and seek for answers to that which you don't understand, or what doesn't make sense." Then they went on to say this, "But when you ask your questions, do so with an open mind, and a teachable spirit. And remember, this side of heaven you may not get answers to all the questions you have about life and death matters."

The Desire To Know Why

When life hurts, when tears flow, it's natural to ask "why?" We'd like answers to questions like: "Why her? Why him? Why me? Why now? Why this? Why doesn't God miraculously intervene?" This is exactly how the biblical character Job responded when calamity hit his world.

In the space of a few short days, Job lost almost everything – his oxen, his donkeys, his sheep, his servants, his sons and daughters, his health—tragedy hit Job out of nowhere and left him with a lot of unanswered "why" questions: "Why didn't I die at birth? Why do people like me, who seek to live a righteous life, suffer? Why do the wicked grow old and increase in power? Why have you made me your target? Why are you hiding your face from me?" Honest heartfelt questions posed by a really nice guy who was deeply hurting.

I wish I could tell you Job got answers to his questions. He didn't. Four of his closest friends tried their best to answer his questions, but in the end their responses were pathetic. Deemed by God as foolish. Their simplistic approach that suggested his calamity was due to personal sin didn't hold water. Sure his pain was ultimately connected to life in a world wracked by the consequences of sin, but in this case this man who was called blameless and upright wasn't suffering because of personal sin that if confessed would make everything okay again.

Near the end of the book, God speaks to Job and his friends, through a barrage of penetrating questions like: "Where were you when I created the heavens and the earth? Can you comprehend the vast expanses of the earth? Who provides food? Does the eagle soar at your command? Now what do you have to say for yourself? Are you going to haul me, the Mighty One, into court and press charges?"

Where To Run

Questions, questions and more questions. All unanswered. Enough to make you wonder what's a person to do when life doesn't make sense and it leaves you with a series of unanswered questions. When that happens to you, which I am sure it will if it hasn't already, I'd urge you to respond like Job did. Go ahead and ask your questions but in the end make sure you run *to* God rather than *from* Him.

"In this world," Jesus said, "you will have tribulation." We wish it weren't so. But that's the way life is (thank you Adam and Eve). And with tribulation comes a choice. A choice to turn to God or away from Him. Job chose the later. In the midst of pains and tears he was able to say, "Naked I came into the world and naked I shall leave. Blessed be the name of the Lord." (1:21) Though he didn't understand the "why" behind the "what" he went through, He believed God was in control. Trusting the maker of the heavens and the earth was better than the alternative. Job was even able to say, "Though He slay me, yet I will trust Him" (13:15) because as Job said, "He knows the way that I take and when He has tried me I shall come forth as gold" (23:10).

Job realized what he was going through was for a good purpose. Like a goldsmith who melted gold over a fire that the dross might rise to the surface and then be removed, he believed God was doing the same in his life. And like a goldsmith knew the gold was pure when he was able to see his reflection in the gold without any impurities, God was perfecting Job that all might see the Lord through him. That fact gave Job hope in the midst of his unanswered questions.

Not "Why" But "What" And "Who"
When I was in graduate school I got an unexpected phone call from one of my brothers telling me that my mother had just died. I was utterly shocked as was our entire family. Mom had been feeling sick and complained of a few aches and pains, but none of us, including her, knew she was dying of cancer at the young age of forty-two. I had a great mom. She loved the Lord and her family dearly. She was a devoted Christian. She prayed daily, worshiped regularly, served constantly. She loved to teach Sunday School and Bible Study Fellowship. Mom was just a great all around person. Not perfect, but genuinely sincere in her commitment to Christ.

That's why it was so hard to understand her death. "Why mom? Why now? Why did she of all people die at such a young age?" These were just a few of the questions that puzzled us. In the midst of our questioning, a pastor from our church came over to offer his support and comfort. We were grateful for the things he shared, but mostly I was thankful for the words he prayed. I'll never forget them. Before he concluded his visit, he gathered all of us as a family in the living room of my parents' home and prayed for us. I can't remember all that he said, but I do remember this. He prayed,

"And Lord help them not ask *why* this has happened, but *what* it is that you want to do in and through them in the days ahead."

When life hurts, it's natural to shed tears and ask why. Allow yourself room for both as you work through your grief. But I'd also urge you to run *to* God and not *from* God. To the one who can be trusted even when you don't know the *why* behind what you're going through. Trusting in *who* God is, and *what* He wants to do in and through your life, will give you comfort and hope when you don't have a clue about the *why*.

Let yourself cry and ask why

Even though you, like Job, may never get an answer to your why questions, you can live with hope and comfort when grieving.

What questions right now would you like answers to?

How can the following verses be an encouragement to you now and in the future?

Job 23:10 – But he knows the way that I take; when he has tested me, I will come forth as gold.

Psalm 17:3 – Though you probe my heart and examine me at night, though you test me, you will find nothing; I have resolved that my mouth will not sin.

Psalm 66:10 – For you, O God, tested us; you refined us like silver.

James 1:2-4 – Consider it pure joy, my brothers, whenever you face trials of many kinds, because you know that the testing of your faith develops perseverance. Perseverance must finish its work so that you may be mature and complete, not lacking anything.

If you never get an answer to your why questions, this side of heaven, will you still be able to trust God and believe that He always does that which is best?

PART NINE

SPIRITUAL COMMITMENTS

twenty-five

Dependence
Loving God 24/7

IF YOUR JOURNEY to independence is anything like mine was, your parents spend a lot of time on their knees praying and hanging onto hope that you'll make it safely to adulthood. And soon! The day I turned 18 and declared I was an adult, my parents breathed a huge sigh of relief. And then they quickly took me up on my declaration of adulthood and independence.

To say I was not an easy child to raise would be putting it mildly. But in my defense, if any of my three siblings had been the first born instead of me, they would have given my parents just as hard a time as I did. And maybe worse. If you're a first-born you understand—we bravely pave the way for the rest of the kids in the family!

The rocky road leading up to my declaration of independence was filled with many out-of-control but now-kinda-funny experiences. All brought to my family at my expense. And they love telling those stories now to my kids. In fact, recently while my brother Greg & his wife were up in Montana on vacation with all of us, he had a great time recounting many of those memories. Including the infamous "learning to drive with the whole family in the car" incident. His story went something like this...

Yeah, I can still remember the time you almost killed our family. And dad almost killed you! (I disagree. I didn't almost kill our family. But the part about dad almost killing me, well...I really did make him very very angry.) *I'll never understand why mom and dad agreed to let you, with just a learner's permit, drive to the gas station with our entire family in the car. I was only twelve years-old but I still remember it like it was yesterday.*

We made it to the gas station fine. But when you pulled up to the pump, Dad realized the station was out of gas or something so he said we would have to go to the one across the street. Instead of going back out to the intersection and waiting for the light, you decided to just go straight across the street. Which dad probably would have done too—if there hadn't been a divider in the middle of the road!! But before he could stop you, you drove out of the station and straight over a six-inch high three-foot wide center divider without stopping!

After you banged the front wheels up over the curb, the bottom scraped its way across the cement island until finally the back wheels made it over and slammed down on the pavement. And of course while all this was happening, dad, who was riding shotgun, was freaking out and screaming, "DAVID, WHAT THE BLANKETY-BLANK ARE YOU DOING?!!! He was so ticked off he probably would have killed you if mom hadn't been screaming, '*LOERING! STOP YELLING AT DAVID! HE'S JUST LEARNING TO DRIVE!!.'* (And again in my defense, they had just put that curb in a few days before my encounter with it. Who knew?!)

I don't think raising me was *always* that challenging—at least that's what I'd like to think. But it wasn't easy. My parents had their own issues. We all do. And they were new at being parents of a kid my age (There's that first-born thing again). And I was new at pretty much everything. Which led to some tough parenting challenges in their quest to see me grow up to become a fully functioning independent adult.

On the Way to Independence

That really is the goal, isn't it? Something your parents have labored for since you were an infant? Helping you grow and mature. That there would be a day when you would sleep through the night. Crawl. Walk. Feed yourself. Use the bathroom instead of diapers. Talk in sentences. Learn to say please and thank you. Obey those in authority over you. Reach your potential in school. Discover your talents and gifts and begin to live them out. Do what's right without being told. Learn to sensibly and responsibly set and keep your own curfew time. Get and keep a job and start saving as much as you can. Learn to drive safely (without driving over dividers). Your parents are seeking all of that and more for you.

This child-raising thing may be a lot of hard work, but it isn't hard to understand. It's meant to be an intentional gradual baton pass. A transition over time. We as parents are simply trying to help you grow up and become a responsible independent adult.

Independence Day isn't just a major motion picture that grossed millions—it's been your destiny and your pursuit. From infancy on it's been the goal. You've been looking forward to the time when you could finally do your own thing. Unobstructed. Without parental interference.

Progress toward that day hasn't been easy for you or your parents. You've shed a few tears (and maybe thrown a few tantrums?) when you didn't get what you wanted. It was tough as a two-year-old being told at night that you needed to stay in your bed and go to sleep. Even now it can be a challenge when asked by your parents about something as simple as doing chores or homework. Either can be hard to swallow when your will is in conflict with theirs. You'd like complete freedom to chose to do whatever you want whenever you want.

You might be surprised to know that parents want that for you too. In fact, like you, they've been dreaming of the day when you're out on your own making your own decisions. They want to see you equipped and prepared to live a mature independent life. Capable of making smart choices that put you on the path to God's best for your life. The thought of you becoming all that God made you to be excites them. They're thrilled for your potential future.

Independence *and* Dependence

If your parents are followers of Christ, your independence isn't their only child-raising goal. They also want you to grow to be dependent. Yes, independent and dependent at the same time. That's when life is at its best. But by dependence, I don't mean on your parents. At the same time that you are growing to become *independent* of your parents, you should be growing in *dependence* on God. If you've read much of the Bible you know that things don't end well for those who choose to live independent of God. "*And every man did what was right in his own eyes*" was always followed by big trouble.

As you transition out from being under your parents' authority there is great potential but also great danger. This could be the best time in your life as you begin to discover who you were created to be. There are so many possibilities ahead of you! New adventures with new paths to explore. And the choices and decisions will all be yours.

But what's ahead could also lead to disaster if you take that new-found independence too far. To assume that you now will have all the answers is to assume wrong. What happened in the story of the Prodigal Son (Luke 15:11-32) could easily happen to you. Well, maybe your story wouldn't involve pigs, but you know what I mean.

In his quest for independence he ended up temporarily walking away from his values, beliefs, and relationship with God. His independence got him into a huge mess of trouble. Which is where the pigs come in. It wasn't pretty.

As you move into this new phase of independence from your parents, I'd strongly urge you to move toward God and grow in your dependence on Him.

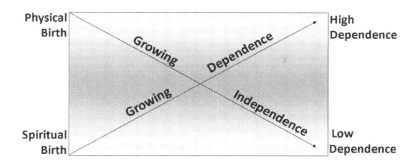

Independence Gone Bad

Unfortunately, recent statistics tell us that two-thirds of incoming college freshman who claim to be born again will no longer make the same claim by the end of their college experience. That's right. Two thirds. Pollster George Barna found that only twenty percent of those who were highly churched as teens remain spiritually active by age 29. That's one out of five!

Why does that happen? There are obviously a number of reasons one could point to. But most, if not all, of those reasons come back to independence gone bad. It's rooted in our basic human desire to do one's own thing, to have it your way, to not let anyone tell you what to do…a young adult turns his or her back on God and walks away. Same story—*"And everyone did what was right in their own eyes."*

Do you recall our brief look at King Solomon earlier in this book? His life can be summarized in three chapters:

> Chapter One – Dependence *(the good life)*
> Chapter Two – Independence *(the wasted life)*
> Chapter Three – Dependence *(the recovered life)*

Solomon really messed up in the middle. He walked away from dependant living for independent living. He thought he'd find a better life if he did it his own way. He didn't. And after getting knocked around for a while, he finally got it. Like the Prodigal Son, he came to his senses and finally said:

The last and final word is this: Fear God. Do what he tells you.
And that's it. Eventually God will bring everything that we do out
into the open and judge it according to its hidden intent, whether it's
good or evil. (Ecclesiastes 12:13-14, MSG)

I've already suggested that you can save yourself a lot of time, effort, money, and heartache by learning from someone else's bad experiences. Well here's another significant opportunity to do that. Solomon, the wisest man who ever lived, came to realize through his own bad experiences that the best path to success and happiness is in living a life that is vitally connected with and dependent on God.

- Maintaining a sense of holy awe toward the God of the Universe.

- Honoring and respecting Him.

- Worshiping Him for who He is and what He's done.

- Abiding in His Word.

- Showing your love for Him by obeying His commands and teachings.

An Independent Dependent

All of that requires dependence. And honestly, there really is no better way to live than as an independent person who is dependant on God 24/7. Do you like the sound of that? I do. Connected to the maker and provider of all things. Handing over control to the creator of the universe. Trusting Him to guide you through your life as an independent adult.

Sometime in the not too distant future the first chapter of your life will be complete. Call it "My Dependant Years." A continuum of experiences that God and your parents have guided you through in order to prepare you for the next chapter of your life. I can think of no better title for your Chapter Two than: "My Independent Dependant Life." I hope you agree.

Loving God 24/7

Up to now you've had to depend on someone – a parent, grandparent, guardian, relative – to get you to where you are. What happens next depends on who you depend on from here.

What words describe this first chapter of your life as you've been dependent on your parents?

When you think about being out *on your own*, what excites you? What fears or concerns do you have?

When it comes to your relationship with God, can you say for sure that you are committed to dependant living? What do you think this will look like?

What importance is placed on dependence in this verse?

> *Colossians 2:6-7 – And now, just as you accepted Christ Jesus as your Lord, you must continue to follow him. Let your roots grow down into him, and let your lives be built on him. Then your faith will grow strong in the truth you were taught, and you will overflow with thankfulness. (NLT)*

What things can you do to make sure your roots grow deep into Him so you will stay dependent on Him?

twenty-six

Church
Deliberately get plugged in

WITHIN SEVEN DAYS of leaving home as an 18 year old enjoying his new independence, I was confronted with Sunday, which for the previous 18 years of my life had meant Church Day. My family went to church on Sunday. Had Fresno First Baptist Church given out attendance pins, our family would have received a bezillion of them. We were there every Sunday.

Mom and dad made sure of that. No excuses allowed. And I promise you I exhausted the "unable to go to church" excuse list. Anyone in our family who wasn't currently throwing up or bleeding was told to "Get in the car, we're going to church!" In fact, that was back in the day when "church" didn't just happen on Sunday mornings. We also went through this routine on Sunday nights and Wednesday nights!

As a kid, that meant I had no choice but to be a regular attender of our FBC Youth Group. From what I remember, other than Sue Dahlstrom, Don Ford, and Steve Skinner, everyone else in the group also had little if any interest in church. That was our parents' deal. Had they not forced us to go, we wouldn't have gone. But they did. So we did. Which explains why once we made an appearance at church, most of us snuck off and spent the next hour at a nearby A&W enjoying something that was a whole lot better than a dull boring worship service.

On the Sunday's when one of our parents caught us trying to leave, we were personally escorted into the sanctuary where we then chose to sit at the top of the balcony, as far back as a person could possibly go. With no one behind us we were free to play games—like dots and boxes on the back of church registration cards—or pass notes, or sleep.

Earlier in this book I wrote about my Westmont College shuttle job when I got paid to drive students to the church of their choice on Sundays. I was surprised to find that the overwhelming majority, even at a private Christian College, didn't go to church—unless *Bedside Baptist* or *Church of the Inner Spring* qualifies. After being forced by my parents to go all those years, and my dislike of church as a child, you'd think I would have been among Westmont's church drop-out crowd. Surprisingly, I wasn't. And honestly, it wasn't just because I was getting paid to go!

Something Happened Last Sunday

Have you discovered the uncanny fact that you hear things even when you're not listening? I discovered that unusual reality one Sunday while tuning out the service from my perch in the balcony at FBC Fresno. I was in the service, but not really in the service. At least that's what I thought.

Something in me must have been paying attention to the pastor's message because all the sudden I heard him say "I gotta go now." With twenty minutes yet to go in his message, my uninterested mind somehow knew those four words were out of place. I looked up from my game of dots and boxes just in time to see him pass out and drop like a brick on the floor. All of a sudden, for the first time, I took an interest in church. Ushers and leaders rushed to help him while an Associate Pastor urged us all to pray—which even I did. Later that day we got the news that he was okay and church would continue as normal the next Sunday. Oh joy. The excitement was over. Back to boring. Or so I thought.

As expected, my family and I were back in church the following Sunday. They sat downstairs, I sat upstairs. But this Sunday for some reason I actually listened. On purpose. Maybe it was just curiosity to see if the pastor would do it again. Fortunately that didn't happen, but something unexpected did.

That Sunday something in me began to take an interest in church. Slowly, gradually, what I heard in the worship services started to find its way into my soul. And not just me, but several others in our youth group too, as the truth of God's Word began to penetrate our defenses and transform us.

Totally Unexpected

By my junior year in high school I had gone from dreading church to actually looking forward to it. I started to bring a Bible. I soon forgot that A&W was just across the street. And a few of us from our youth group even led a pew relocation drive. We vacated the back row of the balcony and started sitting in the second and third rows on the main floor, directly in front of the ginormous pulpit. All to the shock of our parents. We even began taking notes of the message!

My enthusiasm for church that began in high school didn't stop once I was out on my own. During my first two years in college, even though I was living out on my own, I continued to faithfully worship at the same church my family attended.

But the real test came when I moved out-of-town and away from my family and our home church. If I didn't go to church on Sunday, they'd never know! It would have been easy, like the majority of others I knew, to bail on church. And I could have built a good case for it since I was attending a Christian College where we had to go to chapel services twice a week, and we had way too much homework to get done.

But my momma didn't raise no church drop-out.

Honestly, the thought of leaving church, after leaving home, never even crossed my mind. To me, abandoning church would have been like ignoring someone I cared deeply about. Why would I want to stay away from someone that I loved and wanted to be with? Well I somehow felt that way about church.

Now don't get me wrong. I don't for a second believe a person has to attend a worship service at a local church to worship God. Such a belief contradicts the clear teaching of the Bible when it says to offer our bodies "as living sacrifices, holy and pleasing to God – this is your spiritual act of worship" (Romans 12:1b). Everyday we worship God wherever we are by honoring Him with all that we are. Our day-to-day walk with God is what should be the center of our worship and of our Christian life. That's expected of a faithful Christ follower, as is believers coming together to encourage each other and worship the Lord together.

Reasons to Plug In
If you're on the fence about the importance of taking the time to meet with other believers for corporate worship, for gathering with God's family on a regular basis, I'd urge you to consider three very important matters. I think of them as the *upward, inward,* and *outward* factors of worship.

When you gather with others for worship you have the opportunity to *exalt* God together (upward), be *encouraged* by others (inward), and *evangelize* any unbelievers who are there. Any one of those three things is reason enough for a person to make it a priority to gather with God's people regularly.

I find it amazing that God *seeks* our worship (John 4:23). Jesus called it what's "most important" when He told Martha, who was worried and bothered about getting a meal ready, that her sister Mary, who was worshiping at Jesus' feet, was doing what mattered most. When we set aside our day-to-day lives and sit at Jesus' feet and genuinely *exalt* God, the Lord is honored and we are supernaturally changed by God and each other. Transformation, edification, and encouragement happen.

In the years shortly after Jesus' death and resurrection, believers were told to "consider how to stimulate each other to love and good deeds, not giving up meeting together, as some are in the habit of doing, but encouraging one another..." (Hebrews 10:25).

They, like us, needed ongoing encouragement as they lived out their day-to-day lives for God. So they were admonished to continually meet up with other believers to encourage each other.

It's a lot easier to be a Christian today than it was back then. But it's still hard to live our lives day-by-day for God. It's not easy to actually put into practice loving God and loving others. And when you add to that the fact that this fallen world is filled with pain and suffering, and it will be until Christ comes again, you realize that we live with the same need for encouragement and support from fellow believers as those early Christians did. Like football players who huddle to plan, strategize, support, and encourage each other so they can get back out in the game and win, believers must gather on a regular basis to do the same.

And let's not leave out evangelism. When the church gathers, she should expect unbelievers to be present (1 Corinthians 14:23-25). When the body of Christ genuinely worships God in ways that even an unbeliever can understand, the Word of God through the Spirit of God can have a life changing impact on the lost. The corporate testimony of the church can be a key ingredient in a person coming to faith in Jesus Christ (John 13:34-35).

At a minimum, regular times of fellowship with other believers gives us an opportunity to exalt God, encourage each other, and evangelize unbelievers. Once I came to see these three reasons for worship, I had all the incentive I needed to keep time with other believers a priority in my life. I pray the same for you.

Check List to Consider

If you do make a commitment to worship regularly with other believers, you may find it challenging to find a church to plug into. Here are a few things that could be helpful as you look…

1. *Pray for the Lord's guidance:* God is more than willing to lead you to the best church for you. Ask Him to show you His will and He will.

2. *Check out churches online:* You can learn a lot about a church before ever attending. Check out their history, statement of faith, leadership, sample messages, etc. If you have

practical, leadership, or theological questions, ask some of them by way of email.

3. *Attend a few worship services:* One may not be enough. Some things to think about while you're there: Is the service prompting you to focus on God and worship Him? Does your mind and heart connect with the music? Is the Word of God explained and applied in the Pastor's teaching? Do people really worship in this church or are they just going through the motions? Would you love coming back?

4. *Seek to be friendly:* Give yourself and others the best possibility of connecting. Don't just arrive at the last minute and leave right away when the service ends. Make time to hang out a little before and after the service. Are there signs that you will be able to connect in meaningful ways with others here?

5. *Consider opportunities to serve:* Would there be a place for you to serve? Would you want to serve there if you could?

Shortly after I arrived in Santa Barbara for college, I did what I am encouraging you to do. I began to pray and look for a church to attend. It took a month or so to find the one I felt God wanted me at, but the time I spent looking was well worth it. I found a great church. It inspired my worship, encouraged my faith, and the Lord was bringing unbelievers to Himself through their ministries. For the two years I lived in Santa Barbara, Calvary Church had an important role in my life. I still have some of the notes I took as I sat under Pastor Geshew's teaching. His messages in the book of Galatians were especially important to me. And his explanation of the fruit of the Sprit in Galatians 5 was life changing.

I love the church. The Bible says she's the bride of Christ. I can't imagine trying to do life apart from her out on my own.

Deliberately get plugged in

Now is a good time to stop and think for a few minutes about your commitment to the Body of Christ, the Church.

How would you describe your commitment to other believers to date? How about to worship at a local church? On a continuum of 1-10 (ten being high), how strong has your commitment been to meeting with other believers for times of worship and encouragement?

When you leave home, are you planning on leaving the church behind? Why or why not?

In what ways can the following verses help you be among those who faithfully worship the Lord?

> *1 Chronicles 16:29 – Give to the LORD the glory he deserves! Bring your offering and come into his presence. Worship the LORD in all his holy splendor. (NLT)*

> *John 4:23-24 – "But the time is coming—indeed it's here now —when true worshipers will worship the Father in spirit and in truth. The Father is looking for those who will worship him that way. For God is Spirit, so those who worship him must worship in spirit and in truth." (NLT)*

twenty-seven

Impact
Making an eternal difference

IT'S ALL ABOUT ME. For my first 15+ years, my life revolved around me. Which in one respect is true for all of us. We are each technically the center of our universe. But some of us take it to a whole new level. And that is not a good thing. Some of us don't think much about anyone else. It's all about me.

That's how my life began. And I might have stayed that way if it weren't for the fact that when you grow up as part of a church family, you have the opportunity to get to know some great people – like the three Rons who left an indelible impact on my life.

Ron Eckert was the choir director at our church. When I was in high school the church music scene started to change all across the country, and Ron changed with it. Christian composers and musicians began writing youth choir musicals which Ron introduced to our church.

Though it was hard for some of our older church members to embrace those drum-driven, guitar-mixed songs, Ron saw their value and led the charge to start a youth choir that pulled self-centered teenagers like me into volunteer ministry. Before I knew it, I was involved in a newly formed youth choir that we called The Eternal Trip (seriously, but hey, it was the 60s!).

We had practices through the school year to learn everything, and then for a week in the summer we'd jump on a bus and go on tour to Rescue Missions, prisons, Rehab Centers, malls, amusement parks, you name it. We'd sing and then a few of us would share our testimonies. It was an awesome way to witness to unchurched people.

Serving Can Change Your Life
Before that I had never experienced the excitement of going out and doing ministry. Though I have to admit that at the time that wasn't my motivation for singing with The Eternal Trip. To be honest, I was in it because that week we were on tour away from home. And there were a lot of cute girls in the choir! Those choir tours were a blast.

But in the midst of all the good times we were having on those trips, God got a hold of my heart and gradually began to change self-centered Dave into a new and better Dave. I started to put serving others above always thinking about myself. That was a big change. And with it came a whole new excitement and desire to help people that I had never really even thought about before. On those choir tours I was exposed to a lot of people who were really in need—physically, spiritually, emotionally, relationally. And it rocked my world and got me looking out the window at a world in need rather than into a mirror at myself.

The second Ron was Ron Neufield, our High School Youth Pastor. He was also key in God's work to change my heart. Ron had a simple idea of starting a weekly volleyball night at our church in the summer for high school students. Instead of pulling this outreach activity together by himself, he asked if I would take it on and organize the promotion, court, teams, and food. For some reason I said yes and God used that experience to give me an even greater desire to help others. Plus, as I served, God began to show me I had organizational and leadership gifts that I hadn't known about before.

And then there was Ron Dangaran. By the time he came onto the scene, as our second High School Choir Director, I was fast becoming a student leader with the choir and youth ministry. And I was also amazingly becoming someone whose heart was growing soft. My desire to help others in need was growing large. Ron #3 affirmed and encouraged that by giving me even more opportunities to show God's love to others in practical ways. And he even got me speaking before crowds of people, which accelerated my desire to see others connect with Christ in significant ways.

I Can't Stop Doing This

By the time I got to college, my passion for ministry was rapidly increasing. It had become so much a part of my life that when I finished my two years at City College I actually wasn't sure if I wanted to attend Westmont and finish a 4-year degree. I was already working with a youth group, there were needs to be met, and ministries to be run. Did I have time to go on to finish college?

As I was deciding if I should go to Westmont, a book titled *The Late Great Planet Earth* came out and rapidly became a best seller and gained worldwide popularity. The book focused on Christ's second coming and predicted He could come very soon. I was stoked!

It also got me thinking that the last place I wanted to be when Jesus came back was in college and out of ministry. Wouldn't it be better to be out there right then helping people who needed to get things right with Jesus before He returned? I wasn't sure I wanted to waste two years away at a Christian college.

Fortunately, God led me to a solution that allowed me to do both college and ministry at the same time. It turned out to be great for me, and my college experience was enriched by my ongoing outside commitments to ministry. During those two years at Westmont I made time for helping with a Sidewalk Sunday School ministry, counseling at a drop-out prevention center, and leading a weekly campus Bible study at Santa Barbara City College.

Those ongoing ministries filled my desire to be ministering to others. And as an added bonus, all of those hands-on ministry experiences equipped me for what came after I finished college. Plus my résumé turned out looking really good.

To this day I owe a debt of gratitude to all three Ron's who had a positive impact on my life. It was their belief in me that got me into ministry. I am deeply grateful.

Saved to Serve

If you're already involved in activities or ministries that are making a difference in others' lives, I commend you. I hope you're seeing much fruit come from your efforts and sacrifice. I also hope your heart is flooded with the joy that comes to those who live as investors rather than consumers.

Service is at the heart of God's plan for His children. You see that in Bible passages like:

> *Ephesians 2:10 – For we are God's workmanship, created in Christ Jesus to do good works, which God prepared in advance for us to do.*

> *Matthew 5:16 – In the same way, let your light shine before men, that they may see your good deeds and praise your Father in heaven.*

> *Col. 1:10a – And we pray this in order that you may live a life worthy of the Lord and may please him in every way: bearing fruit in every good work…*

> *1 Tim. 6:18 – Command them to do good, to be rich in good deeds, and to be generous and willing to share.*

> *Hebrews 10:24 – And let us consider how we may spur one another on toward love and good deeds.*

> *Titus 3:14a – Our people must learn to devote themselves to doing what is good…*

From his very first day of ministry, Jesus had one thing on His mind. Servanthood. Which in His world, like ours, was completely contrary to the thinking of the day. While everyone else was putting themselves first, Jesus modeled a life of service. Of putting others first. Of meeting others' needs.

And He called His followers to that same kind of life when he told them, "…whoever wants to be great among you must be your servant" (Matthew 20:26b). Jesus was the best servant ever and He mandated that those who follow in His footsteps should live lives of service too.

When Small is Large

The life of servanthood often begins with a willingness to do the little things. Are you good at serving in little ways? Like taking out the trash without being reminded? Or helping hand out bulletins at church on Sunday mornings? Or maybe working as a volunteer at Vacation Bible School? Or helping a local food bank sort food?

At some point I came across a verse that transformed my thinking about the importance of wholeheartedly taking on the small stuff. Found in Luke 16:10, Jesus said, "Whoever can be trusted with very little can also be trusted with much, and whoever is dishonest with very little will also be dishonest with much." Simply stated— those who are faithful with the little stuff can be trusted with the big stuff. God gives bigger responsibilities to those who've demonstrated faithfulness with the little things.

If you're like the rest of us, you want to do something significant with your life. Something that really matters. Something that will have a positive impact on others. You'd like to make your life count.

As is often the case, knowing which path to take toward that kind of impact is key. That's where Luke 16:10 comes in, which I believe holds the secret to great impact. If you want to see God do great things through you, be great with whatever God's given you *right now*. That may mean taking on something that seems too insignificant or "below you." But in God's plan it may be a test or the means by which He prepares and trains you for greater responsibility in the future.

The Path To Great Impact

Little did I know that my faithfulness in organizing a weekly high school volleyball game (including setting up and taking down the net each week!) would lead to greater ministry opportunities. But it did. For over forty years now God has opened door after door for me to have greater impact opportunities. But not without my faithfulness in the ministry responsibilities He gave me along the way.

I never thought I'd end up as a Senior Pastor. But God knew, and He gave me many opportunities along the way to show Him I could be trusted with Lead Pastor responsibilities. One of those came with a youth ministry assignment in Agoura Hills, California that I had no interest in. But I took the position because I believed God opened the door and wanted me to walk through it. Little did I know at the time that walking through that door would take me through several other doors which ultimately led me through a really big door where I'd become the Senior Pastor of that same church. For twenty-one years I served in that role all because I said "yes" to the first little door God opened.

If you want to be a person of impact and reach your God-given potential - start serving. Be willing to do the small stuff. Prove that you can be trusted. When God opens a door for ministry, walk through it. Do your best. It could be the beginning of something bigger than you ever thought possible.

Making an eternal difference

Take a few minutes and think about what we've been talking about.

In what ways to date have you been involved in ministry and service to others? What words would you use to describe your experience?

Take another look at these three verses. Personalize them. Do you in the core of your being believe God wants to use you in acts of service and impact?

> *Ephesians 2:10 – For we are God's workmanship, created in Christ Jesus to do good works, which God prepared in advance for us to do.*
>
> *Matthew 5:16 – In the same way, let your light shine before men, that they may see your good deeds and praise your Father in heaven.*
>
> *Hebrews 10:24 – And let us consider how we may spur one another on toward love and good deeds.*

Where do you see God opening doors of ministry opportunity for you right now?

If you were to walk through those doors, or others behind them, what kind of impact would you hope for? God only knows what your future holds, but now's as good a time as any to say, "Lord, here am I. Use me."

PART TEN

PRACTICAL TIPS

twenty-eight

Home Stuff
Master the basics

WHEN I WALKED OUT of my parents' home to begin life on my own, I was clueless as far as what was actually necessary to successfully live life on my own. In looking back, I can see I needed a lot more training. I knew how to cook Kraft Macaroni & Cheese, so I wasn't going to starve, but that was about it. I ate a lot of macaroni & cheese. And when I wanted some variety I chopped up a hot dog and stirred it in.

The beginning of life on my own was rough, kind of like my early days in Boy Scouts. The first time I took a three-day two-night backpack trip with my troop, I loaded my pack with cans of soup, stew, and pork & beans. I must have been lugging an extra fifty pounds on my back because of those cans. But my mom and I wanted to be sure I had plenty to eat.

You should have seen my Scoutmaster's eyes when he saw me pulling the kitchen pantry out of my sixty-pound backpack. He was not a happy camper. Talk about an embarrassing moment. To put it nicely, my mom and I had a lot to learn about being *appropriately* prepared for camping and backpacking. What seemed like a good idea while I was still at home packing, ended up making my trip a lot harder because my backpack was way too heavy!

Moving out of your parents' home to live life on your own, whether in a dorm or an apartment, is similar. The reality of it is a lot harder than you might think if you're not prepared. There are probably a lot of things that get taken care of in your parents' home that you take for granted. *Somebody* just does them. But once you're out on your own… you'll quickly realize that you're that somebody! And if you don't do them, they won't get done.

Things like cleaning—dust and dirt and scum are not your friends. And laundry—eventually you'll run out of clean clothes. And grocery shopping—the days of the magic refrigerator that's always full are over.

If you want to survive and thrive when you're out on your own, you need to acquire and equip yourself with some essential homemaking skills. And the time to do that is now, before you leave home. Don't wait until the day you run out of clean underwear to try to figure out how to run a washing machine. Just saying…

What follows are four areas I'd urge you to add now to your list of homemaking skills so you'll be prepared to live on your own. And so you'll be eating more than just 101 variations of macaroni & cheese.

Cleaning Your Home

Some people are clean freaks. Others avoid cleaning like the plague. You've probably already figured out where you fall on the cleaning continuum—unless you're like my son's friend Robbie. He had a brother that was a couple years younger than him and they shared a bedroom as they were growing up. Robbie was always complaining about how their room was so messy because of John. But when Robbie went off to college—without John—after about a month of living in a dorm room, he realized *he* was the messy one!

Home cleaning can be an endless chore. It can include straightening things up, dusting, vacuuming, mopping floors, sorting through piles of stuff, putting things away, taking out the trash, washing the dishes, cleaning the bathroom (including the toilet), washing windows, etc. If your mom was like mine, it could even include washing the walls every couple of weeks!

It will be up to you to decide where you're going to fall on the clean freak/slob continuum. Once you're out on your own it will be your choice. Most of us fall somewhere in the middle. But if any of those chores are going to get done, you're going to need to be the one to do them.

If you're open to suggestions on how to make that happen, here are my top three:

1. The easiest way to keep your room/house clean is by living with a "clean as you go" mindset. If something spills… clean it up right away. If you use a plate, fork, and glass…stick them in the dishwasher or wash them instead of just throwing them in the sink for later. If you mini-task today, it will keep you from having to do everything later all at once.

2. When faced with specific cleaning tasks (laundry, vacuuming, cleaning bathrooms, etc), do the hardest things first. It will make what is yet to be cleaned seem easier.

3. Set a time limit for major cleaning days. This is especially important if you tend to be easily distracted. If you tell yourself, "For the next 60 minutes I will clean as much as I can" and then do it, you'll feel great with whatever you accomplish. Just make sure that the next time you clean you start with the things that you didn't get done the last time.

Doing Laundry

Unless you plan on wearing the same clothes over and over, or buying new clothes whenever you run out of clean stuff, you're going to need to do laundry. Some of you may have been doing your own laundry since middle school, but others may have a mom who does it all. So here are a few helpful suggestions that could make doing laundry easier.

o   It's best to separate your dark clothes (things that could fade) from your white or light clothes. This will keep your white clothes from becoming the color of your dark clothes. If you purchase a clothes hamper with two or three sections, you can save some time by separating your dirty clothes right after you wear them.

o   When washing whites, use hot water. When washing dark clothes, use cold or warm water. Using cold water will prevent color fading.

o   Get into a laundry routine. Pick a day and time every week to do laundry. Doing that will keep you from having to do a mountain of laundry at one time, and it will get done faster.

o   If you'd like to minimize and in some cases avoid wrinkles, pull your clothes out of the dryer as soon as the dryer stops. And then don't leave them all shoved in the laundry basket to be put away later. Hang them up and put them away right away. Dryer sheets can also help...and they make your clothes smell good.

o   If your clothes are stained, apply a stain remover as soon as you notice the stain. Stain removers can be purchased at the store in the laundry aisle. Whatever you do, if a stain does not come out after washing the garment, do not put it in the dryer. First repeat the stain removal process or try getting the stain out another way.

Chef You

Some people love to cook, and others… not so much. I personally think the difference is directly related to their cooking competence. Aside from macaroni & cheese and waffles, I'm not very good in the kitchen. When my wife is out of town, I usually just eat out. Fast food is so easy, and fast. So I was lucky to have married young. If I had stayed single longer I probably would be very unhealthy and way over weight today thanks to a steady diet of Round Table and In N Out and Taco Bell.

There are a lot of books out there that can easily teach you the basics of cooking. And there are a ton of resources online. Find something that's easy to read and start experimenting in the kitchen. You don't have to be Julia Child or Rachel Ray, but it would be a good idea to know how to scramble eggs or bake potatoes.

On top of my cooking incompetence, I was also a very picky eater for years. Which meant unless it was some kind of meat or potato —preferably French fries—I took a pass. But recently my eating habits took a drastic change once a nutritionist started teaching me about a healthy diet. I'd heard the basics before in school, but knowing and doing are two different things. I guess this time I was finally ready to do. The bottom line – everyone would do well to eat more fruit & vegetables & protein & whole grains, and limit sweets and processed foods.

Have you ever considered the importance of your body from God's perspective? The Bible tells us your body is God's temple. God resides in you. That makes your body of significant value to God. It's His will that we glorify Him with our bodies. In fact we are also told to glorify God by what we eat and drink.

So get out there and eat to God's glory. And while you're at it, do what you can now to acquire the skills needed to be a great shopper and cook. Your body will love you for it, and you can even honor the Lord through what you prepare and eat. If you make an effort before you leave home to acquire a decent level of cooking competence, you'll have everything to gain and nothing to lose – in the right ways of course!

Money Matters

Unless your parents, grandparents, or a rich uncle are planning on taking care of you financially, you're going to need to be ready to deal with some money matters. This can be a major headache or a lot of fun as you steward the financial resources God entrusts to your care. If I were you, I'd want to be money smart in several areas:

o   *Setting up and living within a budget.* If you have income coming in, you need a budget. Your personality will determine if this is a set of vague guidelines (like the Pirate Code) or a detailed list of specific expenses. But either way, you need to have at least some idea of how much money you need to cover your fixed expenses, which will then let you know how much you have left to spend at will. At the very minimum you should start by simply making a list of all your fixed expenses – rent, insurance, utilities, food, gas, cell phone, etc. Anything that you know you're going to have to pay regularly. Make sure to include giving and saving in that list too if those things are important to you. Then compare that to your income and you'll have a good idea of how much extra you have to work with. Doing so will help you live within your means.

o   And to take it one step further, there are some very easy but helpful software programs for keeping track of your budget. That's a great way to make sure you don't waste money that you should have saved for bills that have to be paid.

o   *Making a firm commitment to stay out of debt if possible.* As I already suggested, you may not be able to avoid taking on school debt, but you can avoid going into debt over In N Out or a night at the movies. Trust me, those things will add up fast! And you can easily end up with a huge credit card debt and nothing to show for it.

o   *Keeping control of your checking account.* Ever since banks started offering debit cards that can be used instead of checks, banks have been making a ton of money through overdraft charges. I'm guessing that you've probably already felt the pain of those. It's so easy for us to just slide that card to buy stuff without thinking about the limited resources behind it. You need to have some way of keeping track of not only how much money is in your account but also what that money is needed for. (See *budget* above) At the very least, make sure you sign up to have your bank let you know when you get below a certain amount in your account. And once you get that text from them, *stop sliding that card* until you get more money put in your account. I'd suggest you keep a buffer of $100 in there and have the bank let you know when you go below that. Debit transactions aren't always immediately taken out of your account, so it's easy to go over if you're simply checking your balance and assuming the money will be there.

A lot more could obviously be said about money, food, laundry, and house cleaning. My goal in this chapter is only to surface some of the home matters you'll face and offer a few insights worth considering.

Hopefully I've motivated you to get better prepared in each of these areas. A lot of information can be found online. You may be able to pick up one or more classes in school that can help you (and they'll probably be easy A's too!). There are also a lot of books related to these things. However you do it, make sure you take the time now to prepare yourself for living on your own. It could make a huge difference in your future living conditions.

Master the basics

Now is the perfect time to take in as much last minute home preparation training as you can. Here are a few questions that you'd do well to consider.

How prepared are you for the four essential household responsibilities considered in this chapter?

- House cleaning?

- Doing laundry?

- Cooking?

- Money management?

What can you do in the days ahead to better equip yourself in each of these key areas?

- House cleaning?

- Doing laundry?

- Cooking?

- Money management?

How do the following verses speak to the importance of being ready to take on essential household responsibilities?

Luke 14:28-29 – Suppose one of you wants to build a tower. Will he not first sit down and estimate the cost to see if he has enough money to complete it? For if he lays the foundation and is not able to finish it, everyone who sees it will ridicule him,

1 Corinthians 10:31— So whether you eat or drink or whatever you do, do it all for the glory of God.

twenty-nine

Your Car
Minimum maintenance required

PRETTY MUCH EVERY teenager dreams of the day that they'll have their own car. They can hardly wait for the freedom that will come with being able to grab their keys, jump in the driver's seat, crank up the stereo, and go wherever they want, whenever they want.

Some of you who are reading this already know the thrill of having your own car. Maybe you're one of the lucky ones who found yours out in the front yard wrapped with a big bow on your 16th birthday. Or maybe you saved up money from odd jobs for years so you could buy your first car as soon as you got your license. Or maybe you've been gifted grandma's old Impala.

Most of you are probably still waiting for the day when you'll be able to get a car of your own. But eventually pretty much all of you who live in the United States will join the ranks of car owners— complete with insurance payments and car repairs and oil changes and new tires and gas. And more gas.

So I'd like to pass on a few car ownership tips that could be helpful. I've learned a lot over the years since I got my first car. As

I mentioned earlier, I was in the group that worked odd jobs so I could save enough money to buy a car as soon as I was old enough to get my license. Owning that first car was an absolute blast, but also a pain.

Not long after I bought that first car, I discovered that a lot of those sayings we hear all the time are actually true. Like the one that says—you get what you pay for. The car I could afford with the money I had saved up was in desperate need of tender loving care. It had issues. So I enrolled in every Auto Shop class Hoover High had to offer. We actually got to work on our own cars in class so it was a great way to get it running and date-worthy. Both were important.

There were so many things about that car that needed to be fixed. It was really frustrating. But in looking back I can see that the things I learned about cars while I was fixing up that old Ford Falcon have benefited me to this day. It's actually helped me over the years to keep the cars I've owned in good working condition. Not that I've done all the repairs myself. There are mechanics for that. But I do have a good understanding of car care basics that has prevented major car problems and insured safety and dependability in our cars over the years. And there are even some things I've been able to take care of myself.

I hope the same for you, which is why what follows could be extremely helpful. Even if you never take an Auto Repair class, using a simple checklist like the following can help you avoid costly repairs down the road and add years to the life of your car.

Car Care Checklist

☐ **Tires:** Every 6,000 to 7,500 miles it's a good idea to have your tires rotated from the front-to-back or side-to-side. A car repair shop or tire dealer will know exactly when and how this should be done.

For safety's sake, you'll want to keep an eye on the depth of your tire tread. Most states require by law that a tire have at least 2/32" of tread remaining. You can use a penny to measure if your tires have at least this much tread. Simply insert a penny into your tire's groove, with Abraham Lincoln's head upside down. If you can see all of Lincoln's head, your tread depth is less than 2/32" and it's time to replace your tires.

You'll also want to check, or have checked, your tire pressure with a tire gauge (these can be purchased at an auto parts store). The recommended tire pressure (called PSI) can usually be found in the owner's manual (in your glove compartment), or on the inside of the driver's door, or on the side of a tire. The typical recommendation is around 30-32PSI. Inaccurate pressure can cause poor gas mileage, uneven tire wear, and possible blow-outs. It's a good idea to check tire pressure once a month.

☐ **Windshield wipers:** These are often neglected yet are essential to your driving safety. If you can't see out your window clearly when it's raining or snowing, you could put yourself and others in danger. Most car experts say windshield wipers should be replaced every 6-12 months. If your wipers are streaking, failing to wipe consistently, or are noisy (chattering), it may be time to purchase some new ones. First check the wiper blades for tar, dirt, sap, or the like. It's possible that cleaning your blades with a good cleaner and a wet clean cloth may be all they need. However, if they still streak after cleaning, it's probably best to replace them.

☐ **Check engine light:** If one of the warning lights found on your dashboard comes on, your car may have a problem. I know that sounds pretty obvious, but you'd be surprised at how many people just ignore those little lights. If your check engine light comes on, your car may be in need of immediate attention—especially if the light is flashing. When this happens, it's always best to get your car checked out ASAP to prevent possible damage.

☐ **Fluid checks:** According to Consumer Reports, a car owner should regularly check five fluid reservoirs found in your car's engine compartment. If you are not sure where each of these are found, I'd suggest you ask someone so you can check these five fluid levels at least once a month, usually at a time when your car engine is cold.

1. *Engine oil* – Cars come with an oil dipstick (yes, there really is something called a dipstick!) that measures the level of oil in your engine. Once you find this dipstick, remove it and use an old cloth of some kind to wipe the end clean. Then reinsert the dipstick all the way into its sleeve and pull it out again. Look at the end of the dipstick to see how far up the oil comes. A close look will reveal whether or not the amount of oil in your car comes up to the mark and is at a safe operating range. If not, add or have added the proper amount. Like you need blood, your car's engine needs oil to survive.

2. *Coolant* – This is often called antifreeze and is usually found in a clear plastic container near the radiator. On the side of this reservoir you can typically find "full when hot and cold" markings. If the liquid in this container is below the recommended minimum fluid level line, refill with the recommended antifreeze (found in your Owner's Manual). Doing so could keep you out of the "car stopped beside the road with the hood up and steam coming out of the engine" crowd.

3. *Power steering fluid* – This is kept in a small clear plastic container on the firewall which is the wall that separates the engine compartment from the driver's compartment. This level should be kept between the minimum and maximum amounts.

4. *Brake fluid* – This also is typically found in a clear container marked with minimum and maximum lines. If you find this level below the recommended minimum, there could be a leak in the system. If that's the case you could lose your breaks. If this is low, it would be best to get your brakes checked.

5. *Windshield washer fluid* – Of the five fluids to check, this one is least important. But it's also good to keep this

reservoir full in case you need to use it to get your
windshield clean.

Your attention to these five fluids could make the
difference in keeping your car running and safe. Fluid
awareness will also boost the confidence you have in your
car's condition and reliability. If you'd like more info about
these five fluid checks, check out the helpful video found at
http://news.consumerreports.org/cars/2008/12/car-care--
-five.html

☐ **Suggested service and maintenance:** Car manufacturers
recommend specific services and checks at various mileage
intervals. A simple check of the recommended frequencies
found in your Owner's Manual may save you hundreds of
dollars. For instance, 3000 miles or every three months is
the usual frequency suggested for an oil and oil filter
change. Yet General Motors, Honda, and Mercedes Benz
with certain cars and conditions say it may be possible to
wait until 7,500 to 10,000 miles before getting an oil change.
In addition, the car filter manufacturer, Castro, says an oil
filter may only need changing once every 30,000 miles.
Getting your cars oil changed is important, but maybe not
as often as Jiffy Lube would like you to think. When you do
take your car in for an oil change, ask what other services
are included in the cost of your oil change. Often this can
include: inspecting and topping off your fluid levels
including your battery, checking your tire pressure and
adding air if necessary, inspecting your engine belts,
windshield wiper blades, and exterior lights. Depending on
the make or model of the car you own, additional service or
maintenance checks are suggested at other frequencies like
15k, 30k, 60k, 90k, 120k, etc.

☐ **Safety and appearance:** Owning a car is a tremendous
privilege and an ongoing responsibility. It's a big investment
so take time to care for your car. Keep an eye on your car's
condition. Little matters like small chips in the windshield, if
taken care of sooner rather than later, can keep a small
problem from becoming a big one.

☐ **Car log:** It's a good idea to keep a maintenance record. Include oil changes, battery replacements, tire rotations and tire replacements, tune-ups, and major repairs. Some people even record every gas purchase (I'm not saying you should, I am just saying…). Whatever level of detail you choose to give to a car log, it really can be a helpful record in your quest to keep your car running well and in knowing what it's costing you to do so. It's generally believed that financially the best car to own is the one you already have. Meaning, it's cheaper to fix your car than to go out and buy a new one. But if you find you're spending a ton of money just to keep your car running, then it might be time to trade it in.

A Great Privilege, A Great Responsibility

At first glace, the above list may seem intimidating and overwhelming. Enough to make you say, "What have I gotten myself into?" Cars can be a pain with flat tires, and check engine lights coming on, and brake lights going out. But if you take the time to learn some basic car maintenance, and stay tuned in to what's going on with your car, it'll help relieve a lot of the frustration associated with owning your own car. And you can focus more on all the good things that come with car ownership.

One of the nice things about owning a car is that you don't have to know a lot to enjoy its benefits. A little bit of knowledge, like that given in this chapter, can go a long way in multiplying the benefits your car gives you. And when something isn't right, or something goes wrong, there is a huge car repair industry around you that can help.

When that time comes, and it will, here's a final tip. Take your car to a mechanic that is ASE certified. ASE stands for Automotive Service Excellence. In order for an auto repair shop to be ASE certified it must employ one or more service professionals who have passed one or more of the 40+ intensive tests covering various automobile repairs. ASE was established to give a consumer confidence in high-quality and reliable car care.

Not long ago I was sitting in the waiting room of an Auto Repair

Shop while my car's brakes were being replaced. A 20-something woman was also waiting for her car. I asked her why she brought her car to that particular place. At first she simply pointed at the Blue ASE seal affixed to the front window of the shop. Then she said, "My dad owns an automobile repair shop. He told me that while I was away at college, if I needed to get my car repaired, I should take it to an ASE certified shop. I found this place a little over a year ago when I came here for college. They do a great job so whenever I need something done on my car, I come here. I trust them."

I hope the same for you. May the care you give your car, along with the others you enlist on your car care team, lead to many years of car ownership enjoyment.

Minimum maintenance required

Whether you have a car or not, give some thought to the following questions which concern the whole matter of possessions.

So whose car is it anyway? Even if your name is on the pink slip, what do the following verses teach you about ownership?

Job 41:11b – Everything under heaven belongs to me.

Psalm 24:1 – The earth is the LORD's, and everything in it, the world, and all who live in it.

If God owns it all, what role are you to play?

Luke 16:10-12 – "Whoever can be trusted with very little can also be trusted with much, and whoever is dishonest with very little will also be dishonest with much. So if you have not been trustworthy in handling worldly wealth, who will trust you with true riches? And if you have not been trustworthy with someone else's property, who will give you property of your own?"

1 Corinthians 4:2 – Now it is required that those who have been given a trust must prove faithful.

If you were to adopt the above perspective, how would it change what you do or don't do with God's car?

What more can you do to be the best property manager of God's car that you can be?

thirty

Safety Matters

Better safe than sorry

AFTER OUR DAUGHTER Katie finished college she got a job as a flight attendant. I think her mom and I probably loved her job even more than she did. The family perks were great! Like flying free on her airline or only paying $25 to fly anywhere—yes, anywhere!—on other airlines. I think Katie would say, "My parents were the benefactors, I was the laborer." And that was just fine with us.

As a flight attendant Katie had to deal with a lot of weird things, including first time flyers, rude know-it-all frequent flyers, seating issues, baggage problems, customers locking themselves in bathrooms, weather delays, the smell of smoke, the smell of gas (seriously), electrical issues, and of course the fear of flying. Not hers…others. Including *my* fears for Katie. I did my fair share of praying for her safety as she flew back and forth across the United States in all kinds of weather conditions, and drove back and forth to LAX (where she was based) at all hours of the day or night.

Whenever we flew on our daughter's airline, the pilots and fellow flight attendants treated us great. Since their planes didn't have first-class seating, their kindness usually translated into a smile, some affirming words about our daughter, and maybe a free snack or drink. While all of that was nice, the one thing I valued more than anything else came out of a conversation I had one day with a pilot. After asking him a question about challenging flying conditions, he reassured me that foremost in a pilot's mind was *flying safe*. Hearing him say that was music to my ears as a passenger, but mostly as a protective dad who loves his daughter and cares about her safety.

Safe Thinking

Today when I travel, *fly safe* frequently comes to mind. A couple weeks ago Bernice and boarded a plane bound for San Jose, CA from Austin, TX. At first everything seemed okay. The plane pushed back from the gate on time, taxied out to the runway like normal, and then waited for clearance to take-off. But when it was our turn, instead of moving onto the runway, our pilot turned the other way and brought the plane to a stop.

After a minute or so of wondering what was going on, the captain came on the intercom and said, "We have a problem we need to attend to." My first thought was that I was glad he was saying that while the plane was still on the ground rather than at 35,000 feet in the air! He had my full support to take whatever time he needed to fix the problem to insure we'd *fly safe*. Our plane ended up delayed for a couple hours and then we were safely on our way.

Growing up with two brothers, I must have heard our mom say "Boys, be safe!" a million times. But in spite of her warnings, we were constantly doing stuff that was anything but safe. Like the times we tied bath towels around our necks, climbed up on the roof, and leaped off Superman Style. Fortunately it was just a one-story house! When mom caught us doing dumb stuff like that she'd scold us and tell us never to do it again and then speak one of the international cardinal rules of safety, *"It's better to be safe than sorry".* Which is right up there with *"It's all fun and games until somebody loses an eye!"* But usually we'd just continue on our merry way, still believing we were invincible.

Those warnings became a vivid personal object lesson the day we all took our last Superman dives off the roof. Both of my brothers, and I am not lying, broke an arm that day. Mark jumped first and landed on his right arm. He ran into the house screaming and crying and in a lot of pain, while Greg and I just watched from the roof. Greg then took a flying leap that ended up being his last Superman flight. I guess he thought he should hurry while mom was busy with Mark so he'd be down before she came out to yell at us. He landed on his left arm and broke it. Now I'm not stupid. I quickly realized the odds weren't in my favor that day so I carefully climbed down from the roof.

Be Safe Not Stupid

My kids would add in a third safety phrase that they heard a lot from their mom. Often when she said "Be safe" they would reply that they weren't planning on doing something stupid and getting hurt. To which she would reply, *"No one ever plans to have an accident! That's why they call it an accident!"*

If your parents are like mine were, or like we were with our kids, you've also heard *"Be safe!"* a bezillion times. And you've probably learned through experience (broken arms?) that it could also be translated *"Don't be stupid!"* So by this time do you have a safety first, don't be stupid, instinct hardwired into your brain? Parents like me would breathe a huge sigh of relief if we knew you did.

In the near future you are going to be leaving home. That means your parents aren't going to be around to remind you for the millionth time to *"Be safe."* So from that point on it will be up to you to choose how safe you're going to be. [I must insert here that once my kids went off to college I didn't worry as much about them…mainly because I didn't have a clue what they were actually doing at any given time!] The choice will be yours. What kind of risks will you be taking, either consciously or simply because you're not thinking about it?

Two Types of Risk

Risk is often divided into two kinds: controllable risks and uncontrollable risks. *Controllable risks* are those you can do something about like locking doors and windows; choosing not to walk alone at night; not talking or texting on your phone while driving; not leaving valuables laying out in the open; not getting drunk; not getting in a car with a stranger or someone under the influence of alcohol; leaving a light on when you're out late at night; not driving around alone in dangerous places; not jumping off the apartment balcony into a pool. These would fall into the "Just don't be stupid" category.

Uncontrollable risks could include anything from driving home for Christmas break, to eating dinner out with friends. Both of those things seem like normal experiences that shouldn't be much of a problem. But it's wise to remember that some things are out of our control. Like Bernice used to tell our kids, you don't plan for accidents to happen.

I have a college friend who was killed while driving home to Fresno from Westmont for Christmas break. He was on a two-lane road in the middle of nowhere at night when the driver of a car coming from the opposite direction lost control and swerved into his lane. Both he and his girlfriend were killed instantly.

The risk of getting food poisoning doesn't even compare to Ben losing his life in a car accident, but it's another kind of risk that's out of our control. When my college suite-mates found out I had never eaten Chinese food before, they took me out to dinner at the China Palace in Santa Barbara. I considered the possibility that I might not like my dinner (remember, I was a meat and potatoes kinda guy), but it didn't even cross my mind that I would end up with a bad case of food poisoning. That was not fun.

Safe Risk Taking

Life is filled with risks. Unfortunately, because we live in a fallen world there are dangerous situations all around us. Accidents waiting to happen. But we don't want to hide in our dorms afraid to go out and live our lives. We need to find a balance. And sometimes we need to simply trust God when we feel He's calling us to do something that could be risky, like going on a missions trip to China or Africa. Or feeding the homeless in an inner city park.

It's okay to take risks. In fact God calls us into that kind of life, but we can also be smart about how we live. If you're going to feed the homeless in a sketchy area, make sure you go with a group and dress in a way that won't draw too much unwanted attention.

My concern here isn't to talk you out of taking risks; it's simply to ask you to seriously consider the level of safety you are committed to in controllable areas of life. By now you're old enough to have learned that you're not Superman. Take time to stop and think about what you're doing. Whether those areas pertain to physical, emotional, mental, or relational aspects of your life.

Even the Bible speaks about issues of safety in light of risk. For instance, the following verses warn against hanging out with certain kinds of people.

> *Proverbs 20:19 – A gossip betrays a confidence; so avoid a man who talks too much.*
>
> *Proverbs 22:24 –Do not make friends with a hot-tempered man, do not associate with one easily angered.*
>
> *Proverbs 23:20 – Do not join those who drink too much wine or gorge themselves on meat.*

When Risk is Too Risky

Some things just aren't worth the risk. Like hanging out with gossips, people with hot tempers, drunks, or even gluttons. Each can have a bad affect on your life. So Solomon, as a father who was concerned for his son's safety, advised him to *avoid, not make friends with, not associate with, not join* people like these. The risks of doing so simply weren't worth it.

Sounds like your parents, doesn't it? "Don't talk to strangers," they said when you were little. "And whatever you do, don't accept a stranger's offer to give you a ride in their car." Sound advice. The risk is too risky. It's better to be safe than sorry.

If you look on-line you can find a number of safety tips worth taking to heart. Tips like these five:

1. *Walk with a friend.* It's less likely something bad will happen if you're with someone else. And if you do have to go out

alone, make sure you are familiar with the landscape. Familiarize yourself ahead of time with the location and its surroundings. Then when you go out, be vigilant and alert to who and what is around you.

2. *Keep your eyes and ears open and your hands free.* Talking on a cell phone or listening on headphones makes you easy prey for a predator. You need to hear what is going on around you. Try to limit the number of items you carry. Put your stuff in a single backpack, purse or bag. This will allow your hands to be free to defend yourself if necessary.

3. *Be extra careful when out at night.* If at all possible never use an ATM at night. Try to only walk in well lit areas. Switch your routine. Get in the habit of taking different routes if possible.

4. *Let someone know where you are going.* A buddy system is for adults too. If you're going somewhere you don't want people to know about, perhaps you shouldn't be going there.

5. *Take care of yourself.* Get plenty of sleep. Try to eat healthy. Find time to exercise. Practice the art of saying no. Especially when someone wants you to do something that you know could be harmful.

Be Safe Not Sorry

To be honest, I hadn't originally planned to include a chapter on safety in this book. But as I was meeting with some parents to talk about what I was writing and to get their input, they asked if I could include a chapter that would encourage their kids to "Be safe!" So I will end this book, and this chapter, by reminding you that there are a lot of dangers out in the world. Some you can control. Some you can't. And some that God may even purposely lead you into.

Be safe. Be smart. Don't be stupid. In how you choose to drive. How late you stay out at night. Who you hang out with. Where you go. What you do with your body. Will you give it your best effort to *be safe?* The choice is yours, but it seems to me that moms really do know what they're talking about. *Better safe than sorry.* Right?

Better safe than sorry

Some of you are overly cautious and may need to learn to take a few more risks. Others are right there with me jumping off the roof in a Superman cape. Take a few minutes to consider some questions that can help you *be safe*.

Some people are risk avoiders, others are risk takers. Where do you land on the risk continuum?

In what specific ways are you committed to safety? List some of the things you will or won't do for safety's sake? Are there some things it would be good for you to change about your choices right now?

Living in the midst of an unsafe world can be hard. How do the following verses calm your heart?

Hebrews 13:5b – "Never will I leave you; never will I forsake you."

Deut. 31:8 – The LORD himself goes before you and will be with you; he will never leave you nor forsake you. Do not be afraid; do not be discouraged.

Psalm 91:11 – For he will command his angels concerning you to guard you in all your ways.

Seriously...*just one more thing*

WHEN I LEFT HOME at the age of 18 to go out into the world on my own, my life was all about me. I could do what I wanted when I wanted and how I wanted. It was great! I had been waiting for that day for a long time. Oh I had to navigate relationships with roommates and co-workers and friends and girlfriends, but for the most part I was living free and easy as a single guy. It wasn't until I got married five years later that I realized how self-centered I was.

Sometimes I really have to wonder why Bernice even married me. I'm thinking if we had lived together before we got married, like the overwhelming majority of couples do today, it's doubtful she would have said "yes" when I proposed! I guess I should be thankful that back in the day only the fringe of society (like those hippies!) lived together before they got married.

I can still remember the morning when my focus on "me" became painfully clear. At the time we were living in a very small home that had one bathroom with one sink. Since I tend to wake up early and Bernice believes God created us to sleep until the sun comes up, I usually used the bathroom first to get ready for the day. On that fateful morning I did my usual routine, which involved a lot of soap, shaving cream, and water, before Bernice got up. Then I turned the bathroom over to her.

I guess on that morning Bernice had finally had enough. When she woke up she took one look at the bathroom and then called me back in there. Then she said something like, "Dave, have you ever noticed what a mess you leave in the bathroom? Does it ever even cross your mind to clean it up a little when you're done? Look at this!" And I looked. And she was right. There was water and shaving cream splashed everywhere on the counter and the mirror.

Then she added, "Would you want to find the bathroom like this when you come in?" ugh She said it so sweetly but it was like a punch in the stomach because *I'm* the one that is really picky about stuff like that!

You've heard of the Golden Rule, right? It's one of those things that we all learn in Kindergarten. It's actually recorded in Luke 6:31 when Jesus said, "Do to others as you would have them do to you." Sounds good, doesn't it. Sounds easy. Treat others the way you want to be treated. You want respect? Show respect! You want to be treated fairly? Treat others fairly. You want a clean sink? Leave a clean sink!

The concept of the Golden Rule transcends religions and cultures. Confucius said, "Do not do to others what you do not want them to do to you." The Hindu faith teaches, "This is the sum of duty: do naught to others which if done to thee would cause thee pain." The Jewish Talmud declares, "What is hateful to you, do not to your fellow men. That is the entire Law; all the rest is commentary." The book of Tobit, found in the Apocrypha states, "Do not do to anyone what you yourself would hate." Even the bottom line of secular culture in America today could be summed up as "Everyone has the right to live however they want as long as they're not hurting anyone else."

Similar ideas, but did you notice the difference from God's perspective? Other cultures and religions put the emphasis on not doing bad things to other people. Which is a good thing. But Jesus took it beyond that. It's not just about not hurting others, but it's also about helping others. Doing good things for them. The kind of things that you would want done for you.

Jesus said that the bottom line of life should really be all about love. Loving God. Loving others. That's it. If you don't remember anything else from this book, remember that. If you can get that down you'll be on a great path toward a great life as you leave home.

Then He also tells us that the proof of our love for God will be whether or not we love others. Not by simply saying we do, or by feeling warm fuzzy emotions, but by our actions. If we love God, we will love others. We'll be other-centered instead of self-centered. We'll treat them the way we want to be treated. We won't treat them badly and we'll go out of our way to treat them well. We'll be living examples of the Golden Rule.

Actually that puts us right back where we started in this book - with the importance of making the right choices. It takes a deliberate choice to live your life loving God and loving others. To live out the Golden Rule day by day. To leave others better off because your life touched theirs. And it's a choice that you'll need to continue to make day after day and year after year.

As you head out into the world in the near future, my prayer for you is that you will wake up each morning and choose to live that day for God and to show His love to anyone who may cross your path. If you will do that, and then do it again the next day, and the next... you will be amazed at the adventures He will lead you to and through as you follow Him.

ABOUT THE AUTHORS

Dave and Bernice met in high school in Fresno and then went to Westmont College together in Santa Barbara. Shortly after Dave graduated they got married at the very young ages of 22 and 21. Bernice finished her degree in Psychology at Fresno State while Dave worked as a Youth Pastor. They then moved to the Los Angeles area so Dave could get his Masters at Talbot Theological Seminary (the graduate school of Biola). Their parenting years began a few weeks before Dave graduated from Talbot as the first of their three children was born. Just a few months later Dave became the Lead Pastor of Agoura Bible Fellowship. For the next twenty-one years Dave and Bernice learned how to pastor and parent as ABF and their family grew. During that time Dave also earned a Doctorate from Western Seminary in Portland, Oregon.

When their two sons were out of the home and attending a SoCal college, Dave & Bernice & their daughter Katie moved to Phoenix, AZ as Dave became the Lead Pastor at Bethany Bible Church. During their time in Phoenix, both of their sons married California girls. And when their first grandchild was born—and Dave & Bernice became Grandpa & Nonna—God gave them the green light to move back to California so they could be closer to their kids and grandkids.

Today Dave and Bernice live in the Bay Area where Dave is the Lead Pastor at Bridges Community Church in Los Altos. They are actively involved in the lives of their family as they try to be the best parents and grandparents possible to their five grandkids. And there are more to come!

Along the way, Dave has also hosted a weekday radio program, taught seminars for Walk Thru the Bible, and written three previous books—*Owner's Guide to Using Your Bible*, *Before You Live Together*, and *Before You Get Engaged*. He'd tell you he couldn't have done any of that without Bernice by his side.

Also available from **David Gudgel**

Helps couples who are thinking about living together know if doing so is the best thing for them now and as they look toward their future as a couple.

Read it for yourself. Read it with the one you love. Read it to make the right decision when it matters most. This book is also an excellent tool for pastors, counselors, and anyone who is in a position to give advice to singles.

Helps couples who are thinking about getting engaged know if they are ready to offer or accept a marriage proposal.

In *Before You Get Engaged*, authors David Gudgel, his son Brent, and Brent's girlfriend Danielle give practical advice that will help readers know if they are ready to get engaged, if they should date a little longer, or if they should end the relationship and move on.

Made in the USA
Monee, IL
16 July 2024